For

my mother
Dorothy Stiles Gillespie
1918–1995
who flavored her fare with inimitable flair

my grandmother
Myra McCord Stiles
1890–1967
*whose cornpones we still try to replicate
and whose life we still try to emulate*

my great-grandmother
Emma McCord
1851–1925
teenth-century recipes for living have made all the difference

Keepin
and Ho
T E

The How

Your Great-Great-

whose nine

Keeping Hearth and Home in Old TEXAS

The How-To Book

Your Great-Great-Grandmother Used

compiled and edited by
Carol Padgett

Keeping Hearth and Home in Old Texas

Copyright © 2005 Carol Padgett
This edition published exclusively by Sweetwater Press in conjunction with Menasha Ridge Press.

All rights reserved. No part of this book may be reproduced in any form or by any electronic or mechanical means, including information storage and retrieval systems, without written permission of the publisher.

Printed in the United States of America

ISBN 1-58173-479-4

Cover design by Travis Bryant
Text design by Grant M. Tatum and Annie Long

Order online at www.booksamillion.com.

Contents

	Acknowledgments	VII
	Introduction	1
	Chapter One	FOR THE LADY WELL GROOMED AND WELL DRESSED 5
	Chapter Two	FOR THE LADY WELL COMPORTED 21
	Chapter Three	FOR THE YOUNG LADY COURTED AND ESCORTED 27
	Chapter Four	FOR THE WIFE 37
	Chapter Five	FOR THE MOTHER, AS SHE COMFORTS AND CARES FOR THEM 43
	Chapter Six	FOR THE MOTHER, AS INSTRUCTRESS 59
	Chapter Seven	FOR THE NURSE 67
	Chapter Eight	FOR THE HOMEMAKER SETTING UP HOUSEHOLD 83
	Chapter Nine	FOR THE COOK APPOINTING HER KITCHEN 97
	Chapter Ten	FOR THE HOMEMAKER ON THE GROUNDS 105

	Chapter Eleven	FOR THE COOK AT HER TASKS 113
	Chapter Twelve	FOR THE DAILY COOK: FAMILY TABLE RECIPES FOR BREAKFAST, LUNCHEON, AND SUPPER 141
	Chapter Thirteen	RECIPES FOR DINNER: SOUPS AND MEATS 165
	Chapter Fourteen	RECIPES FOR DESSERTS AND BEVERAGES 173
	Chapter Fifteen	COMPANY EXPECTED: RECIPES FOR SPECIAL GATHERINGS 185
	Chapter Sixteen	FOR THE LADY AS HOSTESS 195
	Chapter Seventeen	FOR THE LADY VISITOR, THE LADY CALLER, AND THE LADY CORRESPONDENT 199
	Chapter Eighteen	FOR THE LADY IN MOURNING 209
	Bibliography	213
	Index	221

Acknowledgments

Keeping Hearth and Home in Old Texas took shape at a keyboard rather than a pastry board, with ingredients pulled from library shelves rather than kitchen shelves. Yet, the process of preparing this 19th-century buffet of recipes and "receipts," mores and maxims has been reminiscent of growing up in my grandmother's kitchen.

Any attempt to assign proper measure to those who have assisted me would be as fruitless as my grandmother's efforts to leave her family the legacy of her cornpones. Trying valiantly to render a recipe, she tossed each ingredient into a bowl, retrieved it by handfuls and pinches, and noted its quantity with care. But, alas, there is no measure for a cook's intuition or the size of her palm. Our family has never replicated Ma-Mam's cornpones. We continue, however, to be richly nourished by her spirit. So it is with those who have enriched this effort.

Persons with greater experience in preparing historical bills of fare pointed me to just the right ingredients, hoisted me to the mixing bowl, tended my spills with tact, and helped monitor my pace toward "getting dinner in the oven" on time. Others helped cull my gleanings and arrange the buffet table with impeccable taste. From the other end of our Marital Computer Table, my husband, Ben, added the secret ingredients of perspective and humor; and the family stories of the elders who came with his dowry contributed the leavening of inspiration.

Texas women of the 19th century were my companions and mentors. Their handwritten recipes and published advice provided glimpses into the principles with which they nourished their relationships and the practices by which they ordered their lives. Their quaint language and homespun truths stirred my heart; and our hearthside conversations seasoned my soul. As one of our 19th-century forebears said upon presenting a similar book, "I have enjoyed the task heartily, and from first to last the persuasion has never left me that I was engaged in a good cause."

—Carol Padgett

Introduction

The woman who kept hearth and home in 19th-century Texas was the hub around whom those in the household gathered, from whom they radiated, and to whom they returned. She was the center of the family wheel, assuring its strength with nurture and its stability with constancy. She encircled her family with service—swaddling babies, nursing the sick, and nourishing the well. She was a supportive wife, an encouraging mother, and a welcoming hostess. She followed prescribed forms of her period to tend house and social calendar, children and husband, animals and plants. It is little wonder that a visitor to Texas in the mid-1800s noted not only the tender hearts and gentle delicacy but also the hard work of the state's married women. I have organized *Keeping Hearth and Home in Old Texas* as a guide to fulfilling the functions that kept the wheels of life turning for the 19th-century Texas homemaker and her family.

Keeping Hearth and Home in Old Texas is a lovingly constructed anthology of homemaking advice culled from a wealth of mid-to-late-19th-century cookbooks, household manuals, and periodicals. It is, in essence, a greatest-hits album of the domestic wisdom of the time, a simpler time, a time without (for most Texans) electricity, telephones, automobiles, supermarkets, and countless other conveniences we take for granted today. My passion for capturing the wisdom of this age resides in my lifelong fascination with the everyday lives of those who came before me: What was it like to live then? What were the tasks and pleasures that filled the hours of each day? I have always treasured the old-time literature of the home as a tender personal keepsake, much like the legacy of handwritten recipes and hand-stitched finery that my female predecessors left behind. For me, putting this book together was an opportunity to step into the shoes of my great-grandmother, or even of her mother. I can see them sitting side by side, skimming these pages in search of just the right recipe for calf tongue, a trustworthy treatment for a colicky infant, or the best advice for making fine cologne water in anticipation of a rare night out.

I smiled and chuckled my way through the work of choosing the most representative pieces of advice to include. My mother, grandmothers, and all the great aunts, bedecked in their finest aprons and best memories, gathered in spirit 'round the hearth of my desk to help select ingredients. We laughed at the measures and manners of yesteryear and lampooned the family legends of which they reminded us. Simultaneously 57 and 7, I rejoiced in the reverie of the childhood Sunday dinners that nourished our family with home-cooked food and touchstones of predictability—forks on the left, hands in the lap, elbows off the table, and my grandfather's weekly admonition to "count the silverware before taking out the trash." From the vantage point of my sixth decade, I relived my first: lips puckered to be glossed for a trip to town, eyes wide in search of "ladies" (who "could be spotted a block away by the presence of gloves"). Seventeen once more, I revisited reminders familiar to women of earlier eras: "It is just as easy to love a rich man as a poor man" or "Every young woman needs an education and skills to fall back on *just in case.*"

It is my hope that *Keeping Hearth and Home in Old Texas* will stir your memories and bring the lives of your great- or great-great-grandmothers into the storytelling circle beside your family hearth, for this is how they lived; and this book is one they might have consulted, had such a comprehensive collection been available during their day. Instead, our forebearers consulted a variety of sources, learning about household management from receipts in the addenda of period cookbooks and learning the finer points of proper deportment and social propriety in the designated columns of weekly newspapers and in magazines such as *Godey's Lady's Book, Harper's Bazaar,* and *The Ladies Repository.*

These texts connected women to the broader society and assisted them in examining and shaping their individual lives. In fact, this literature became so extensive that *The Enterprising Housekeeper*, written in 1897, noted that it was "almost the fashion to apologize for taxing a much-abused public with the burden of a new book on this subject." Yet how grateful we should be for the abundance of this literature to educate us about the lives of our ancestors. How I have been humbled by this 19th-century wisdom, for so much of which our 20th and 21st centuries have claimed credit. It seems, more accurately, that women through the ages have agreed on a number of basic principles for orchestrating a home, harmonizing a marriage, and fine-tuning the children. As you shake your head at the quaintness of one practice—*A married gentleman shows respect for his wife by speaking of her as "Mrs." and never as "my wife"*—or feel your skin prickle at the ignorance of outmoded mores—*A lady is at her best when she exhibits a modest and retiring manner*—you will also, surprisingly, often marvel at the modern-day wisdom of other instructions—*Better to live in one room, with all the furniture your own, than occupy a whole house with scarcely a chair or a table paid for.*

Texans have always been pioneers, eager to conquer the frontier of their day. Each decade of the second half of the 19th century presented new frontiers. The 1860s saw the end of the Civil War and the beginning of Texas trail drives to northern markets. The 1870s brought the readmission of Texas into the Union, the beginning of a 100-year Democratic dynasty, and the state's first public higher education. The 1880s belonged to Austin, where the University of Texas opened its doors, as did the present state capitol, which welcomed in 1891 the first native-born Texan governor. Ten years later, Texans crossed the portal of a century in which their state would explore the frontiers of oil, electronics, and manned space travel.

The women who kept hearth and home in 19th-century Texas provided the base camps from which Texans ventured forth to clear pathways to progress. Advice such as that preserved here guided them as they tended the home fires that provided nourishment, warmth, and light for the journey.

There is no doubt that were the rest of the Union to pass from existence, there would yet be left, within the limits of Texas, the elements of a magnificent empire.

—Teresa Vielé, 1858. "A Texas Rose" website.

Chapter One

For the Lady Well Groomed and Well Dressed

Guidelines for Grooming

Be tidy. Young girls, don't allow yourselves to fall into untidy habits. There is nothing more displeasing than an untidy woman, old or young: hair full of dust, shoe buttons pinned on, nails with black rims, clothes ill-fitting—basted and pinned.

Stock your toilet. No matter how humble your room may be, there are eight things it should contain, namely: mirror, washstand, soap, towel, comb, hair-, nail-, and toothbrushes. These are just as essential as your breakfast, before which you should make good use of them.

Set a weekly bath. A set time for each member of the family to take a weekly bath will tend to promote the convenience of the household. Saturday night and Sunday morning are probably the best times for most persons. The weekly bath thus becomes a preparation for Sunday-morning toilet, which is ordinarily the most careful and elaborate of the week.

Use cold water. If begun in summer, there is no danger of contracting a cold from the bath, and as the weather gradually grows colder in fall, no shock will come to the already acclimated system. Then, even though the sleeping room may be so cold that ice forms in the pitcher during the night, the morning bath will be taken without a shudder, and the invigoration and healthy glow which follow will be more than a recompense and reward for the resolution, time, and effort it costs.

Bathe with rain water. Rain water is the best by far to use for the toilet. Little or no soap is needed with it, as it is very soft and easily removes all dirt. In a city house, the best way to obtain rain water is to keep a tub on the roof or in the yard to catch it.

☞ *Pamper Your Body* ☜

- Think deliberately of the house you live in—your body.
- Make up your mind firmly not to abuse it.
- Eat nothing that will hurt it; wear nothing that distorts or pains it.
- Do not overload it with victuals, drink, or work.
- Give yourself regular and abundant sleep.
- Keep your body warmly clad.
- At the first sign of danger from the thousand enemies of health that surround you, defend yourself.
- Do not take cold; guard yourself against it. If you feel the first symptoms, give yourself heroic treatment.
- Get into a fine glow of heat by exercise. Take a vigorous walk or run, then guard against a sudden attack of perspiration.

- ❇ This is the only body you will ever have in this world. A large share of the pleasure and pain of life will come through the use you make of it.
- ❇ Study deeply and diligently the structure of your body, the laws that should govern it, and the pains and penalties that will surely follow a violation of every law of life or health.

—*The Household Guide or Domestic Cyclopedia*, 1898

WASH WITHOUT SHAMPOO. The head should be washed at least once a week, but shampooing is a great detriment to the beauty of the hair. Soap fades the hair, often turning it yellow. Brushing is the only safe method of removing dust from the head, with the occasional use of the whites of eggs when washing

CLEAN THE TEETH DAILY. Cleanliness will preserve and beautify any teeth, unless they are actually diseased. All pastes and toothwashes should be discarded. Do not use the highly advertised preparations, however delightful they are. Chalk and myrrh are excellent and safe dentifrices, as is Castile soap. After using the toothbrush, rinse it in clean cold water and dry it so it is ready for further use.

ALWAYS WEAR GLOVES WHEN:
- ☞ *Housekeeping*. If a lady desires a soft, white hand, she should always wear gloves when performing her household tasks.
- ☞ *Outdoors*. A lady must guard against the elements.
- ☞ *Sleeping*. Sleeping in soft, white kid gloves, after rubbing mutton tallow on the hands, will keep them soft and white. Large mittens worn at night filled with wet bran or oatmeal keep the hands white, in spite of the disfiguring effects of housework.

EAT WELL. Ladies who wish clear complexions, instead of using cosmetics, eat vegetables and fruit, as long as they are in season; and never throw away cucumber water or the juice of any fruit, but rub your face with it whenever you have it.

SUITABLE EXERCISES FOR FEMALES:

Running. To strengthen abdominal muscles, run, lifting your feet high, like a spirited horse.

Skipping. There is prejudice against this form of exercise from the fact that it can be overdone and the idea that it is injurious to girls to jump. If girls are properly dressed, their muscles are gradually developed, and they use common sense, there are practically no dangers in skipping.

Ladies, Go Out. Woman is not a hot-house plant, to be kept indoors under a glass case. She flourishes best when she opens the door and walks abroad, courts the free air and the blessed light of heaven. If this simple philosophy of health were better understood, and such outdoor occupation and exercise were to become a universal habit, we should soon have a new race of American women.

Miscellaneous Recipes—Skin and Face

TO MAKE FINE COLOGNE WATER. Into a bottle, drop the following oils: 1 dram each of lavender and bergamot, 2 drams each of lemon and rosemary, 8 drams each of cinnamon and cloves, and 50 drams of tincture of musk. Cork and shake well.

TO MAKE VIOLET POWDER. Take 12 pounds of wheat starch and 2 pounds of powdered orris; mix together and add a ½ ounce of attar of lemon and 2 drams each of attars of bergamot and cloves.

TO KEEP HANDS SOFT AND WHITE. A French recipe for this purpose is to sleep in gloves filled with a paste made of a ½ pound of soft soap, 1 gill of salad oil, and 1 ounce of mutton tallow. Boil together until thoroughly incorporated. As soon as this is done boiling, but before cold, add 1 gill of spirits of wine and a grain of musk. This is rather a troublesome process, but the result is entirely satisfactory.

> ## Hood's Olive Ointment
>
> ---
>
> CURES:
>
> CHAPPED LIPS AND HANDS,
>
> HARD AND SOFT CORNS,
>
> INGROWING NAILS, BOILS, BURNS, SORES,
>
> SALT RHEUM OR ECZEMA.
>
> CUTS, FLESH WOUNDS, SCROFULOUS SORES,
>
> PIMPLES, TETTERS, FESTERS, ERUPTIONS,
>
> SORE NIPPLES, BROKEN BREASTS,
>
> BRUISES, INFLAMMATION, PILES, CHILBLAINS,
>
> CUTANEOUS DISEASES, ERUPTIONS,
>
> And the hundred and one things for which a good family salve is constantly used. **HOOD'S OLIVE OINTMENT** is prepared only by C.I. Hood & Co. . . . Apothecaries. Laboratory: Thorndike Street, Lowell, Mass. Price 25 cents a box; five boxes $1. Sent by mail, on receipt of price, to any address.
>
> —*Hood's Cook Book Reprint Number One,* 1877

TO CURE MOIST HANDS. Some people have moist, clammy hands that are very disagreeable to the touch. Exercise, plain living, and the local application of starch powder and lemon juice will cure this affliction.

TO WHITEN ARMS. For an evening party or theatricals, rub arms with glycerine, and before the skin has absorbed it all, dust on refined chalk.

TO REMOVE SKIN TAN. An elegant preparation for removing tan is made of a ½ pint new milk, a ¼ ounce lemon juice, and a ½ ounce white brandy. Boil all together and remove the scum. Apply night and morning.

TO REMOVE FRECKLES. Many ladies are very much annoyed at freckles, but we have seen faces on which they were positive beautifiers. Probably the best eradicator of these little blemishes, known as *"Unction de Maintenon,"* is composed of Venice soap dissolved in lemon juice, with oil of bitter almonds, deliquidated oil of tartar, and, after it has turned to ointment in the sun, oil of rhodium. Bathe the freckled face at night with this lotion, and wash the face in the morning with clear, cold water, or if convenient, with a wash of elder flower and rose water. A little lemon juice and milk mixed together and applied nightly will also remove freckles.

Queen Wilhelmina has adopted a custom from the Dutch Indies, and attributes a great deal of the satin-like softness of her skin to the refining and cleansing influence of the lemon baths in which she has indulged for some months, upon the advice of the wife of one of her colonial governors.

—*Recipes for Dainty Dishes: Culinary Toilet and Medicinal Hints*, 1910

On Her Dressing Table

TO MAKE COLD CREAM (which also removes freckles). To 1 ounce of white wax melted in a clean dish, put 1 cup of fresh lard, a ½ teaspoon of pulverized gum camphor, and 1 teaspoon of glycerine; stir well and pour into cups or other molds that have been dipped into cold water. When solid, turn out and wrap in tin foil.

TO FORTIFY AGAINST WRINKLES. The hand of time cannot be stayed, but his marks upon the face need not be placed there prematurely. One of the best local treatments consists in bathing the skin

> ## Seasonal Soaps
>
> **Rice Flour Toilet Soap** is splendid for summer use—mild, wholesome, and elegantly perfumed; just what is wanted to overcome the natural oil which exudes from the body.
>
> **Oatmeal Toilet Soap** is the only perfect winter soap and the cheapest fine toilet soap in the world. If you have never tried it, do so at once. The only genuine Oatmeal Soap is known world-wide as Robinson's Oatmeal Glycerine.
>
> THESE SOAPS ARE MADE ONLY BY THE INDEXICAL SOAP COMPANY AND MAY BE PURCHASED AT ROBINSON BROTHERS & CO. IN BOSTON.
>
> —Advertisement in the
> *Centennial Buckeye Cook Book,* 1876

frequently in cold water and then rubbing with a towel until the flesh is aglow. A little bran added to the water is a decided improvement. This treatment stimulates the functions of the skin and gives it vigor. Wrinkling may be further remedied by washing the parts three times a day with a mix of 4 drams glycerine, 2 drams tannin, 2 drams rectified spirits, and 8 ounces water.

TO MAKE A SIMPLE AND ELEGANT COSMETIC. Take a ½ pound of soft soap, melt it over a slow fire with 1 gill of sweet oil, add 2 or 3 tablespoons of fine sand, and stir the mixture together until cool. Sea sand, sifted from shells, has been found better than that which has no shells. This simple cosmetic has, for several years past, been used by many ladies who are remarkable for the delicate softness and whiteness of their hands, which they in a great measure attribute to the use of it; though they add that they have found common soap, used in the ordinary way, with the addition of the above-mentioned sand at the moment of washing, to answer the same purpose. The cheapness of the above cosmetic forms a strong recommendation of it.

Miscellaneous Recipes—Hair

To cleanse the hair. Break the whites of two eggs into a basin of soft water and work them up to a froth in the roots of the hair. Rinse thoroughly with clean warm water.

Hair-curling liquid for ladies. Take 2 ounces borax and 1 dram gum Senegal in powder; add 1 quart hot water (not boiling). Stir and, as soon as the ingredients are dissolved, add 2 ounces spirits of wine strongly impregnated with camphor. On retiring to rest, wet the locks with the above liquid and roll them on twists of paper as usual. Leave them till morning, when they may be unwrapped and formed into ringlets.

To ward off gray hair. We can only counsel moderation in all those pleasures that tend to an exciting, unhealthy mode of living, but here is a recipe that a writer says she believes will prevent graying: Melt 4 ounces pure hog's lard (unsalted) and 4 drams spermaceti together, and when cool, add 4 drams oxide of bismuth. Perfume to suit

—"The Small Belongings of Dress," 1894

Miscellaneous Recipes—Teeth

To care for the teeth. Salt and water cure tender gums. In the early stages, vinegar will remove tartar, but if it remains too long it has a tendency to loosen the teeth. Never use a pin or any metal substance to remove food that lodges between the teeth. Food and drinks that are too hot or too cold will destroy the beauty of the teeth.

> *When* the hair can be worn perfectly plain and still be becoming, one is counted specially fortunate, but as very few faces can stand this a very short fringe is still worn, which, while it is not tightly curled, is made fluffy. The single curl in the centre of the forehead, so much fancied by French women, has not the vogue of last season. Every one wants to be able to part the hair, wear a little jeweled comb at each side and twist it softly either high or low on the neck, for this is not only the most fashionable, but the most artistic style, and is valued accordingly.
>
> —"The Small Belongings of Dress," 1894

To clean the teeth. Rub them with the ashes of burnt bread. The juice of the strawberry is a natural dentifrice.

To fasten the teeth. Put powdered alum, the quantity of a nutmeg, in a quart of spring water for 24 hours, then strain the water and gargle with it.

To cure foul breath. A gargle made of a spoonful of chloride of lime dissolved in a half tumbler of water will sweeten the breath. Bad breath also can be rendered less disagreeable by rinsing the mouth with Horsford's Acid Phosphate.

To cure specific odors. We wish there were a law to prevent people from polluting their breaths with onions and tobacco when going into mixed company. All the laws of good breeding forbid it. The taint of smoking can be overcome by chewing common parsley. The odor imparted by garlic and onions may be much diminished by chewing roasted coffee grains, parsley leaves, or seeds.

Guidelines for Dressing

Dress for the afternoon. Make it a rule of your daily life to improve your toilet after dinner work is over and to "dress up" for the afternoon. A girl with fine sensibilities cannot help feeling embarrassed and awkward in a ragged and dirty dress and with her hair unkempt should a neighbor come in. Moreover, your self-respect should demand the decent appareling of your body. You should make it a point to look as well as you can, even if you know nobody will see you but yourself.

By seven o'clock Mrs. Gray was in her corner, dressed in black silk, with purple ribbons in her cap, and some fine knitting in her hand. Catherine, a brunette, wore a pink silk fastened with black-velvet rosettes, and with puffed sleeves of black Spanish lace. Clara's dress was white cambric striped with pale green. She wore in her hair sprigs of the pale smilax; an old-fashioned gold chain, with a square, red-jeweled ornament, clasped her slender throat, and long ear-rings.

—"The Tea-Party," 1871

KEEP YOUR UNDERCLOTHING IN PERFECT ORDER. Wear shields, such as the Union Undergarments now so much in use, under the sleeves of every dress; if you perspire much between the shoulders, place a square of light flannel next to the skin to absorb perspiration and keep the body from the danger of sudden drafts.

MEND CAREFULLY. If you have but three calico frocks, you can be as neat as if your wardrobe boasted of silk and satin gowns. Examine every garment when it comes from the wash, and, if necessary, mend it with neatness and precision. Do not sew up the holes in your stockings, as we have seen some careless, untidy girls do, but take in a broad margin around the hole, be it small or large, with a fine darning

> ## Recipe for Good Temper
>
> This celebrated recipe, which has been tested in numerous households with the most satisfactory results, is to be found in no other cookbook, but if strictly followed, is guaranteed to produce a perfectly sweet temper, which will keep in any climate until the next Centennial. It is this: For utility and convenience unequalled, buy only the St. John Sewing machine, manufactured by the St. John Sewing Machine Co. in Springfield, Ohio.
>
> It is simple, light running, and durable. It runs either forward or backward without change of stitch or feed. It has a closed shuttle without holes to thread through. It winds the bobbin without funning the machine. It does the greatest range of work of any machine made. It is what you want.
>
> **RISING SUN IS AVAILABLE FOR 10 CENTS A BAR FROM MORSE BROTHERS IN CANTON, MASS.**
>
> —Advertisement in the *Centennial Buckeye Cook Book,* 1876

needle and darning cotton. Cover the fracture with an interlaced stitch so close as to be strong as the body of the stocking and fine enough to be ornamental. Never let pins do duty as buttons or strings take the place of proper bands.

ALWAYS DRESS SIMPLY. A true lady does not adopt gay and showy colors and load herself down with jewelry which is entirely out of place and conveys a very great anxiety to "show off." Your dress may, or need not, be anything better than calico, but with a ribbon or flower or some bit of ornament, you can have an air of self-respect and satisfaction that invariably comes with being well dressed.

SELECT SIMPLE ACCESSORIES. Never carry coarse embroidered or laced handkerchiefs. Fine, plain ones are much more ladylike. Avoid open-worked stockings and fancy slippers. For special occasions, fine, plain, white hose and black kid slippers, with only a strap of rosette in front, are more becoming. Otherwise, wear thick-soled shoes, and in damp or raw weather always protect your limbs; either wear leggings or an extra pair of stocking legs, put on before you put on the stockings.

SCENT YOUR ACCESSORIES NOT YOURSELF. The scented French glove boxes are sufficient in themselves, sometimes, but if a liquid be used, let it be as sparingly as possible. I only seek to impress upon my lady friends the truth of the old proverb as applied to perfumes: "Too much of a good thing is good for nothing." A handkerchief saturated with coarse eau de cologne or a strong essential oil marks at once a person as possessing very little good taste.

SUIT YOUR BONNET TO YOUR FACE. If one has a long slender face, the bonnet should be arranged to make a soft framing; if one has a broad, full face, the bonnet should be sufficiently large, and its trimmings arranged to give a high rather than a wide effect. Ties should always be worn, even if because of a plump throat they have to be very narrow. Nothing gives a woman quite so ridiculous an air as an unsuitable bonnet.

It is in very bad taste, indeed, to wear bracelets outside of your gloves on the street. Although very many fashionable women wear their bracelets outside of their gloves in the evening, the propriatey of it has always been questioned. Three or four strands of small gold beads make the prettiest necklace for a young girl, unless she should be fortunate enough to possess pearls, which, of course, are specially suited to youth and innocence.

—"The Small Belongings of Dress," 1894

Austin
April 1, [19]91

Of course the bracelet is lovely to me, if you like it. I have great confidence in my sweetheart's taste (ahem!); but really every thing you have selected for me has been beautiful and elegant. The little dainty Aladdin's ring, the sweetest of all.

—Excerpt from a letter from Winifred McCraw
to her betrothed, Patrick Swearingen, in San Antonio

AVOID THE TIGHT BODICE, IF STOUT. The average dressmaker who attempts to make a gown for a stout woman makes it as close fitting as possible—as bare of trimming as can be. Nine times out of ten, even if she makes the sleeves full at the top, she fits them in, after the manner of a glove, below the elbow, so that every particle of flesh on the arm is held down, and the hands are extremely red. The result of a tight-fitting bodice is a red face, consequently the stout woman should not wear one, but instead should select that which, while it fits her well, also permits every ounce of flesh to stay in its proper place.

AVOID THE TIGHT SKIRT, IF STOUT. Equally unbecoming to the stout woman is a tight-fitting skirt, and for that reason one with not only a little fullness around the top but also with a fold or two arranged across the front is advised. The stout woman should remember that trimmings carried up to the shoulder, high sleeves, and bretelle effects all have a tendency to increase the height, and that should be her aim in dressing.

MAKE OF YOUR SLENDERNESS A BEAUTY. Wear a bodice that tends to make your shoulders look broader and a much-trimmed skirt that gives to you height and presence. About your waist there must be no trimming, so that its natural smallness can be brought out.

SPORT QUIET COLORS. New or bizarre colors are considered the privilege of the very young woman. Flaring blues, brilliant greens, glowing pinks, or deep yellows seldom look well on a middle-aged woman. She can always wear rich, deep colors; and that she is being catered to nowadays is shown by the popularity of royal purple, of deep petunia, and of the daintiest grays imaginable. Black and white are always in good taste.

> *Mrs.* L. B. Estes,
> Fashionable Dressmaker
> Ave. D, Hyde Park
> Telephone 520; 2 Rings
> Stylish Carriage Costumes
>   and Evening Gowns
>   a Specialty.
> ***Once a Patron,***
>   ***Always a Patron.***
>
> —Advertisement in
> *The Capitol Cook Book*, 1899

Beware the Corset

> ... the corset or tight clothing can do most damage to the vital organs below the diaphragm. The largest of these is the liver.... When Hiram Powers, the great sculptor, was in this country, he once attended an elegant party, and was observed watching very intently a beautifully dressed, fashionable woman. A friend, noticing his interest, said to him, "What an elegant figure she has, hasn't she?" "Well," said Powers, "I was wondering where she put her liver."
>
> —*What a Young Woman Ought to Know*, 1898

Miscellaneous Recipes—Caring for Clothing

TO KEEP MOTHS FROM CLOTHING. Put a few cuttings of Russia leather in your trunk or wardrobe or sprinkle a few peppercorns, pimento corns, or cloves in the same places.

TO CLEAN LACE. Stretch the lace carefully on a thick piece of wrapping paper, fastening the edges with pins. Sprinkle it thickly with calcinated magnesia, cover with another piece of wrapping paper, and place it under a pile of books or other heavy weight for three or four days. The magnesia can then be shaken off, and the lace will appear like new.

TO CLEAN DOUBTFUL CALICOES. Put 1 teaspoon sugar of lead into a pail of water and soak 15 minutes before washing.

TO CLEAN CREPE, MOURNING, AND OTHER BLACK GOODS. Black dress goods may be washed by observing the same caution as for other colored fabrics, whether cotton, linen, wool, or silk. Use 2 tablespoons ammonia to a ½ gallon of water. Take a piece of black cloth and sponge off with the preparation and afterwards with clean water.

TO TEND STAINS. The principal stains and spots the laundress has to reckon with are tea, coffee, wine, iron rust, ink, paint, tar, grass, mildew, blood, grease, and mud stains. These should all be removed from washable articles before sending them to the laundry. Hence many housekeepers set apart Tuesday for wash day, and take occasion Monday to sort the wash and carefully remove all stains, and sponge, scrub, or dry clean any articles that may require it.

Recommendation for Washing Clothes

If I were to be asked by one who was a new beginner what in my judgment was the best way to secure peace, long life, and happiness in the family, I would first ask, "Have you a clothes wringer?" If not, I would then be ready to give my advice. Taking care to let conscience rule, I would say, "Get as one of the first and most essential things Way's Patent Lever Clothes Wringer," and then give my reasons, which are many:

1. It is the most durable and simple in its construction.

2. Its superiority of rolls.

3. No thumb screws, cogs, or springs to rust and get out of order.

4. Its rolls adjust themselves to any thickness of cloth, from a bed quilt to thinnest lace, merely by the pressure of the foot.

5. Your tub cannot tip over, as it is not fastened to the wringer but on one of the best commodities that can grace a laundry, a bench neat and handy, so that a child can readily work it.

In fact, time nor space would allow the naming of all there is to be said in praise of this, the woman's friend. It has taken the premium and two prize medals at the Cincinnati Exposition, 1873–'74 and first premium at the State Fairs of Ohio. In fact it gives splendid satisfaction. Everybody likes it. It is the common sense wringer.

RISING SUN IS AVAILABLE FOR 10 CENTS A BAR FROM MORSE BROTHERS IN CANTON, MASS.

—Advertisement in *Centennial Buckeye Cook Book*, 1876

Chapter Two

For the Lady Well Comported

Cultivate Personal Carriage and Grace

Carry yourself with grace. The beauties of the charming picture framed by a lady's dress are enhanced by her graceful movement. To walk with style is rare enough, but when it comes to sitting down in a dress properly—well, there are not many social graces equal to that.

Keep your arms from going astray. A question often comes up, not so easily answered: What shall I do with my hands and arms? Some ladies always carry a fan. But you cannot always have one in your hands, so it is better to keep the arms pressed lightly against the sides in walking or sitting. This position for the hands, although a little stiff at first, will soon become easy and graceful. Ladies should never adopt the ungraceful habit of folding their arms or of placing them akimbo.

Cultivate your manners. A lady should:
- Be quiet in her manners, natural and unassuming in her language, careful to wound no one's feelings, but giving generously and

freely from the treasures of her pure mind to her friends.

Scorn no one openly but have a gentle pity for the unfortunate, the inferior, and the ignorant, at the same time carrying herself with an innocence and single-heartedness which disarms ill nature and wins respect and love from all.

Such a lady is a model for her sex, the "bright particular star" on which men look with reverence. The influence of such a woman is a power for good which cannot be overestimated.

FIND YOUR MUSICAL VOICE. The sound of a discreet and well-modulated voice is a power in itself. Cultivate a low, clear tone of voice and an easy conversing manner free of gesticulation. Regular features cannot be cultivated, but a kindly expression can be cultivated and so, too, can a pleasant voice.

Slang phrases seem to be *à la mode* in this 19th century; and they issue from rosy lips which appear almost incapable of such guile. We will not repeat the fashionable slang, thereby, perhaps, spreading its serpent trail more widely, but merely allude to the too frequent repetition of "See here," "Hold on," and "I say," wherewith not only callow school girls, but even young ladies who are of so-called aristocratic tendencies and "out in society," delight to adorn their peculiar phraseology.

—*A Manual of Etiquette with Hints on Politeness and Good Breeding,* 1873

Mind Your Demeanor in Social Exchanges

LIMIT YOUR OBSERVATIONS. A quiet person is seldom disliked, while a noisy one sets the nerves all in motion and at war with each other and causes one to feel, in parlance popular, "like flying." Noise, the disturber, deranges the mental faculties and incapacitates the mind for clear and deliberate thought. A boisterous, loud-talking

> *Her* tongue was impatient to speak . . . but she possessed great discretion, and also a large share of that rarest of all womanly graces, the power under provocation, of "putting on Patience the noble."
>
> —*Remember the Alamo*, 1898

man is disagreeable enough, but a woman who falls into the habit is almost unendurable. Many times have we seen an inoffensive husband tucked completely out of sight by the superabundant flow of volubility proceeding from his wife, who, we like to believe, is by nature intended to be the gentler and restraining element.

RESIST SLANG. The use of slang is becoming unbearable. Girls are unable to express themselves in standard language, and slang is growing more and more vulgar. It used to have the merit of a little wit, even if a poor kind, but now it is often a meaningless jingle; and worse, it often carries a double meaning unknown to the speaker, which draws a smile, often of disgust, to the face of every man present.

BE NOT EXCESSIVELY FRANK. Do not take pride in offensively expressing yourself on every occasion under the impression that you will be admired for your frankness. Speaking one's mind is an extravagance which has ruined many a person.

DO NOT BOAST. In company, do not converse with another in a language that is not understood by the rest. If you chance to use a foreign phrase, don't translate it. It is equivalent to saying, "You don't know anything." Never correct the pronunciation of a person publicly, nor any inaccuracy that may be made in a statement. Boasting of wealth, family, or position is exceedingly silly and tiresome to the listeners.

ALWAYS ACCEPT APOLOGIES. Only ungenerous minds will not do so. If one is due from you, make it unhesitatingly.

Listen. When a "tale of woe" is poured into your ears, even though you cannot sympathize, do not wound by appearing indifferent. True politeness decrees that you shall listen patiently and respond kindly.

Laugh at appropriate times. Don't laugh, when a funny thing is being said, until the climax is reached. Do not laugh at your own wit; allow others to do that.

Use tact when admonishment is necessary. Tact is needed in a friend to show us our weaknesses; also with employers and parents. Many do harm instead of good in their manner of rebuking, wounding instead of rousing the self-respect of those they reprimand!

Resist the urge to gossip. A gossip is more or less malicious and uncultivated; if nothing worse, she is empty-headed. Do not hold up the peculiarities of absent friends to ridicule or discuss them uncharitably. Never speak disparagingly of another or rejoice in another's misfortune; it will be charged to envy. News that is not well vouched-for should not be repeated; else you may acquire the reputation of being unreliable.

Refrain from eyeing over other women. Few observant persons can fail to notice the manner in which one woman, who is not perfectly well bred or perfectly kind-hearted, will eye over another woman whom she thinks is not in such good society, and above all, not at the time being in so costly a dress as she herself is in. Who cannot recall hundreds of instances of that sweep of the eye which takes in a glance the whole woman and what she has on from top-knot to shoe-tie. It is done in an instant. No other evidence than this eyeing is needed that a woman, whatever be her birth or breeding, has a small and vulgar soul.

Treat enemies kindly. If you have an enemy and an opportunity occurs to benefit the person in matters great or small, do good service without hesitation. If you would know what it is to feel noble and strong within yourself, do this secretly and keep it secret. A person who can act thus will soon feel at ease anywhere. If enemies meet at a friend's house, lay aside all appearance of animosity while there and meet on courteous terms.

KISS SPARINGLY. Many times a contagious disease has been conveyed in a kiss. The kiss is the seal of pure and earnest love and should never be exchanged save between nearest and dearest friends and relatives. Indeed, public sentiment and good taste decree that even among lovers it should not be so often indulged in as to cause any regret on the part of the lady should an engagement chance to be broken off. Let promiscuous kissing, then, be consigned to the tomb of oblivion

On the Street

※ Ladies in our country are allowed considerable freedom in receiving and paying visits and can appear in the daytime in all public places unattended by their brothers, husbands, or friends of either sex. They can also attend public exhibitions, libraries, etc., and appear on the promenades alone, but this is not the case either in Paris or London.

※ Walk in an easy, unassuming manner, neither looking to the right or to the left, nor walking too quickly. If anything in a store window attracts a lady's notice, she can stop and examine it with propriety and then resume her walk.

※ In bowing on the street, a lady must merely incline her head gracefully and not her body. But she should always smile pleasantly. It lights up the features and adds a refreshing warmth to the greeting.

※ Do not chew gum on the streets.

※ In passing people on the walk, turn to the right.

※ Do not join forces with three or four others and take up the entire pathway, compelling everyone to turn out for you. Walk in couples when there are several friends in your party.

※ Do not pass between two persons who are talking together.

※ Do not introduce people in a public conveyance. It draws attention to a person and makes him unpleasantly conspicuous.

※ Do not seize hold of a piece of goods which another customer is examining, but wait until she has either made her purchase or passed it by.

※ Do not pass in or out of the general entrance of a hotel but by the ladies' entrance only.

Chapter Three

For the Young Lady Courted and Escorted

While Escorted

LADIES, CARRY SOME ARTICLES. The parasol, when that is necessary as a sun shade, must not be borne by the gentleman unless because of sickness or old age the lady requires peculiar assistance. A lady at a ball should not burden a gentleman with her gloves, fan, and bouquet to hold while she dances, unless he is her husband or brother.

ALLOW THE ESCORT TO ATTEND ALL WHILE TRAVELING. When traveling with an escort, a lady should not concern herself with any of the details of her trip. It is presumed that her escort knows more about traveling than she does, and it will annoy him to be continually asked about the safety of baggage, whether they are on the right train, and numberless other fussy questions that would scarcely be excusable in children. The lady or her relatives should supply the escort with sufficient money to defray all her expenses. Some prefer to have the gentleman attend to these matters and settle the account at the end of the journey, but a strict record of all the items should be kept in this case.

Do not initiate long-term acquaintances on a trip. Feel free to make yourself agreeable to fellow passengers, if the journey will be long, without being misconstrued, but an acquaintance begun on a railway train should end there.

Go upon his arm to the hostess. If a gentleman accompanies a lady to a party or dance, he should always wait at the head of the stairs for her to come from the dressing room, and, descending the stairs first, he will be ready to offer his arm in the hall to escort the lady to the mistress of the house.

Learn the art of the horseback mount. The lady should place her left foot in one of her escort's hands, with her left hand upon his shoulder and her right hand on the pommel of the saddle. Then at a given word, she springs up, the gentleman at the same time raising his hand so that he assists her into the saddle. In riding, he should always keep on her right side.

The following day we started for Houston. Eight o'clock had been mentioned as the starting hour of the train for that locality, but the landlord seemed to think we were hurrying unnecessarily when we entered the carriage at half-past seven. There was no waiting room at the starting point that I could see, and we entered the cars, which stood in a very quiet part of the town (not that there was the least noise or bustle in any of it), and seemed to serve as sitting and dining rooms for passengers, who seemed to act generally as if they expected to stay there for the day. But we left Galveston somewhere toward noon, and since we were all good-natured people, and had become pretty well accustomed to the speed of Southern railroads, we really, in a measure, enjoyed the trip.

—"To Texas, And By the Way,"
September 1871

Dancing

At private dances a lady must not decline the invitation of a gentleman to dance, unless she is previously engaged or does not intend to dance any more during the evening. To do otherwise would be a tacit reflection upon the master and mistress of the house.

At a public ball, however, the master of ceremonies or the floor managers regulate the dancing, and they make many introductions, but should always remember to request the lady's permission to do so before introducing any gentleman to her.

Introductions at such places, one must remember, can, if desired, cease with the occasion. A lady is free to pass her partner of the previous evening, the next morning, without the slightest recognition, and he has no right to feel injured or annoyed.

—*A Manual of Etiquette with Hints on Politeness and Good Breeding*, 1873

LEARN THE ART OF THE BICYCLE MOUNT. The gentleman accompanying the lady holds her wheel; she stands at the left, places her right foot across the frame to the right pedal, which at the same time must be raised. Pushing this pedal causes the machine to start, and then with the left foot in place she starts ahead, very slowly in order to give her companion time to mount his wheel and join her. When their destination is reached, the gentleman dismounts first and appears at his companion's side to assist her; if she be a true American woman, she will assist herself as much as possible.

REST IF FATIGUED. During a walk in the country, ascending a hill, or walking on the bank of a stream, if the lady is fatigued and sits upon the ground, the gentleman does not seat himself by her but remains standing until she is rested sufficiently to proceed.

ACCEPT AID. A lady may accept the assistance of a strange gentleman in crossing a muddy or crowded street; such attentions should be accepted in the spirit in which they are offered and acknowledged with thanks.

While Courted

The essential requisites in a companion which are necessary to insure happiness and a life of devotion are to be found in strength of character, a healthy body, a judicious head, a loving heart, all brought into attune with a high and holy life purpose.

CULTIVATE YOUR TASTE FOR BOOKS. A taste for reading will always carry you to converse with men who will instruct you by their wisdom and charm you by their wit, who will soothe you when fretted and refresh you when weary, counsel you when perplexed and sympathize with you at all times.

The Two Lovers

About the final result of these visits I was not quite clear myself. For, though I knew Josephine was well pleased with the idea that a man so superior in mind and worldly advantages should be led captive by the power of her charms, I was sure that Dr. Houghton was much too grave and old to suit her notions of a lover and that handsome and dashing Phil Singleton, who continued, heaven knows how, to make a greater show of wealth with a few hundreds a year than the doctor with his few thousands, came much nearer to her ideal.

—"The Two Lovers," March 1871

IF YOU DESIRE HIM NOT, TELL HIM SO. If a lady perceives that she has become an object of special regard to a gentleman and does not incline to encourage his suit, she should not treat him rudely; but it is

> ☞
>
> . . . *but* I believe every young woman should have so clear an understanding of human nature as to know that she is playing with a dangerous fire when she allows caresses and unbecoming familiarity. She ought to know that, while she may hold herself above criminal deeds, if she permits fondlings and caresses, she may be directly responsible for arousing a passion in the young man that may lead him to go out from her presence and seek the company of dissolute women, and thus lose his honor and purity because a girl who called herself virtuous tempted him.
>
> —*What a Young Woman Ought to Know*, 1898

not well to let him linger awhile in suspense, and then bring him to the point only to be repulsed. Take an early opportunity to express your ideas upon the subject, in a way which will permit him to discover your sentiments.

BEHAVE SENSIBLY TOWARD HIM. And if you have accepted the addresses of a deserving man, do behave sensibly and honorably, and not lead him about as if in triumphal chains, nor take advantage of his love by playing with his feelings. Do not affect indifference to his presence and comfort, nor yet display too much affection for him, while in the society of others.

LET LOVE AND REASON BE BLENDED. Reason is to love what a pair of spectacles is to a near-sighted man. Let your love be intelligent; mix your affection with brains. Reason enables the little fellow to look beyond the fair face and graceful form of his adored, beyond the festivities of the wedding and the beauties of the imagination, to the domestic fireside, to the kitchen comforts, to pudding, and the cash account. That's what reason conjoined with love will do!

BE EQUALLY YOKED. Marry your equal rather than your inferior or superior. Where there is great disparity—either socially, intellectually, financially, religiously, or in any other respect—disappointment and unhappiness are likely to be the result.

CHOOSE A MAN ONLY SOMEWHAT FAMILIAR WITH WOMEN. A woman should avoid accepting a man who has been particularly successful with women. At the same time, she should look for one to whom woman is not an enigma, and a man of the world and of strong character, so that she may feel sure that when he chose her, he said to himself: "I know my mind; happiness for me lies there."

STRAY FROM SPOILED MEN. A woman should avoid marrying a man who is the favorite of many sisters who constantly dance about in attendance on him. That man is spoiled for matrimony. He will require his wife to bestow on him all the attention he received from his sisters, besides those which he has a right to expect from a wife.

Phillip Singleton, attorney-at-law, was a young gentleman of twenty-three, or thereabouts, whose father had recently "set him up," and whose principal business, as yet, consisted in watching for, and bowing to, the pretty girls who passed by his office, and in waiting for the clients who, as yet, were few and far between! . . . [Singleton] proceeded to inform us that it had been a fine day—unusually fine—and added: "Especially for the ladies, you know; the streets begin to look really charming again; upon my word, the little bonnets and things passing a fellow's office are quite distracting, though I regret to say I missed some of the fairest of the sex today from the throng."

—"The Two Lovers," March 1871

STRAY FROM THOSE TOO GOOD. I should advise you to shun a dragon of virtue like fire: a lady should prefer a dragoon rather. A man

A French engaged couple are never allowed to be one instant alone together before marriage. ... I am so far from advocating this policy for American girls.

Let him pay his addresses to her undisturbed; let him say the sweet little foolish things which stir her heart so deeply, but which might stir your risibles; let him sing his love-songs to her and request her to meet him moonlight alone (alone, you observe!) with such expression as love gives the human voice, without your standing by in grim judgment on his performances, as if he were an opera-singer, and had charged you something for listening to him.

—*Get thee behind me, Satan! A home-born book of home-truths*, 1872

may be good, but he must not overdo it. He who has no wickedness is too good for this world; not even a nun could endure him. Fancy, my dear lady, a man being shocked by you! The male prig is the abomination of the earth, and should be the pet aversion of women.

To the Parents of the Courted Girl

CONSIDER SEXUAL COMPATIBILITY. Sometimes, even where a woman is endowed with fair physical powers and would make a helpful and congenial companion if she were equally mated, in her ignorance she consents to marry a man of great amative powers and of an insatiable sexual nature. The same result is inevitable when a man who is weak or of frail constitution and without powers of endurance marries a woman of strong physical powers and dominant sexual nature, whose sexual longings could not be satisfied except by a man who is equally strong and of like tendencies. Such unions oftentimes result in alienation and estrangement, and sometimes in unfaithfulness.

The Proposal

When the time for the proposal has come, your beloved might well consider these thoughts on how to proceed.

WHEN ASKING THE LADY. The mode in which the avowal of love should be made, must of course, depend upon circumstances. The heart and the head—the best and truest partners—suggest the most proper fashion. Station, power, talent, wealth, and complexion all have much to do with the matter; they must all be taken into consideration in a formal request for a lady's hand. If the communication be made by letter, the utmost care should be taken that the proposal be clearly, simply, and honestly stated. Every allusion to the lady should be made with marked respect. Let it, however, be taken as a rule that an interview is best, but let it be remembered that all rules have exceptions.

> He did not speak for a moment. Then he drew nearer, looked with eager, questioning eyes into mine, and, reaching out his hand to me, said only, "Jenny, Jenny!" And then I put my hand in his, and for a moment he held it silently, yet firmly and tenderly, and, bending over, almost reverently, he touched it with his lips and said: "Darling, I will never hold it carelessly, and never, never let it go."
>
> —"The Two Lovers," March 1871

WHEN ASKING HER PARENTS. When a gentleman is accepted by the lady of his choice, the next thing in order is to go at once to her parents for their approval. In presenting his suit to them he should remember that it is not from the sentimental but the practical side that they will regard the affair. Therefore, after describing the state of his affections in as calm a manner as possible, and perhaps hinting that their daughter is not indifferent to him, let him at once, frankly and without waiting to be questioned, give an account of his pecuniary resources and his general prospects in life, in order that the parents may judge whether he can properly provide for a wife and possible family. A pertinent anecdote was recently going the rounds of the newspapers. A father asked a young man who had applied to him for his daughter's hand how much property he had. "None," he replied, but he was "chock full of days' work." The anecdote concluded by saying that he got the girl. And we believe all sensible fathers would sooner bestow their daughters upon industrious, energetic young men who are not afraid of days' work than upon idle loungers with a fortune at their command.

BEHAVE ADMIRABLY WHILE ENGAGED. On your behavior toward your lover during your engagement will greatly depend the estimation in which you will be held by your husband in your married life. Many a wife has been made to feel the galling chains of matrimony by the husband, who, when a lover, was forced to acknowledge his fair fianceé's powers of torture. And on the other hand, the lover should not strive to annoy his lady love in order to discover whether she possesses a large share of good humor; but he should:

- Ever hold her as the queen of his heart, the only lady to whom his attentions are due.
- While in society make her pleasure and her amusement his first charge.
- Not keep close to her side as though held there by an invisible wire, yet manifest a desire to please her in all reasonable things.
- If he seeks the society of others, first see that she is with those who are friendly and agreeable to herself.

Ah! These Honeymoon Days are Golden Days.

... The skies are radiantly beautiful. The carol of voluminous birds is merry music, and the beating heart keeps time to it. ... But when the honeymoon is over! What then? ... the skies darken and weep out their agony; the birds get sadly hoarse, as if with bronchitis, and the sad heart keeps tune to that.

... Can no fortunate compromise-ground be discovered between the domain of turtle-doves and snapping-turtles? ... Perhaps a courtship of generous length would be a sort of antidote to such immoderate "lovingness." ... A fortunate thing, also, would it be for the husband prospective, if, as a plighted lover, he were compelled ... to see his affianced petulant with pain, or nervously fretful with fever; to see her face woefully distorted with toothache; or, what is worse still, with her false teeth loosed from their moorings and entirely thrown aside. A lover who can stand these heroic tests will not be apt to fail in the day of calamity.

—"Ideal Womanhood," October 1871

Chapter Four

For the Wife

Many a marriage has commenced like the morning, red, and perished like a mushroom. Wherefore? Because the married pair neglected to be as agreeable to each other after their union as they were before it.

TEND TO YOUR LOVE ABOVE ALL. If a man and a woman are to live together well, they must take the plant of love to the sunniest and securest place in their habitation. They must water it with tears of repentance, or tears of joy; they must jealously remove the destroying insects and pluck off the dead leaves, that the living may take their place. And if they think they have any business in this life more pressing than the care and culture of the plant, they are undeserving of one another, and time's revenges will be swift and stern. Their love vows will echo in their lives like perjuries; the sight of their love letters in a forgotten drawer will affect them with shame and scorn. In the bitterness of their own disappointment, they will charge God foolishly, thinking that every plant of love has a worm at the root because they neglected theirs and that every married life is wretched because they did not deserve happiness.

Wife, lean upon him. Be neither vexed nor ashamed to depend on your husband. Let him be your dearest friend, your only confidant.

Wife, attend to him. In matrimony, to retain happiness and make it last to the end, it is not a question for a woman to remain beautiful, it is a question for her to remain interesting. Love feeds on illusions, lives on trifles. Not the slightest detail should be beneath her notice in order to keep alive her husband's attention. A rose on her head, her hair parted the other way, a newly trimmed bonnet may revive in him the interest he felt the first time he met her, nay, the emotion he felt the first time he held her in his arms.

Those blissful hours of courtship! Are they ever forgotten—the hand-pressure at the gate; the strolls under the elm-trees; the snatched kiss under the umbrella on that terrible rainy night? You know. Gracious! Don't I pity the married couple who can't look back on such sweet, fond, foolish pictures as this in memory's magic picture-book!

—*Get thee behind me, Satan! A home-born book of home-truths*, 1872

Expect within reason. Hope not for constant harmony in the married state. The best husbands and wives are those who bear occasionally from each other sallies and ill humor with patient mildness. Be obliging, without putting great values on your favors. Hope not for a full return of tenderness.

Confine jealousy and respect him. You need not be at pains to examine whether your husband's rights be well founded. It is enough if they are established. Pray God to keep you from jealousy. The affections of a husband are never to be gained by complaints, reproaches, or sullen behavior. Respect your husband's prejudices and his relations, especially his mother. She is not the less his mother because she is your mother-in-law; she loved him before you did.

Marriage and Toiletry

Now it may enchant a man once—perhaps even twice—or at long intervals—to watch his goddess screw her hair up into a tight and unbecoming knot and soap her ears. But it is inherently too unlovely a proceeding to retain indefinite enchantment. To see a beautiful woman floating in the deep, clear water of her bath—that may enchant for ever, for it is so lovely, but the unbeautiful trivialities essential to the daily toilet tend only to blur the picture and to dull the interest and attention that should be bestowed on the body of the loved one.

—*Married Love*, 1918

BE CHARITABLE, TOLERANT, AND HONEST:
- Never talk at one another, either alone, or in company.
- Never both manifest anger at once; if one is angry, let the other part the lips to give a kiss.
- Never speak loudly to one another, unless the house is on fire.
- Never find fault unless it is perfectly certain that a fault has been committed, and even then prelude it with a kiss, and lovingly.
- Never taunt with a past mistake or reflect on a past action which was done with a good motive and with the best judgment at the time.
- Never part without loving words to think of during absence; you may not meet again in life.
- Never deceive, for the heart once misled can never wholly trust again.

BE WORTHY OF TRUST AND DEFEND ONE ANOTHER. Once established in your home, preserve its affairs inviolate. You should have no friends save mutual ones, and those should never be made confidants of. Should anyone presume to offer you advice with regard to your husband or seek to lessen him by insinuations, shun that person as you would a serpent. Whether present or absent, alone or in company, speak up for one another, cordially, earnestly, lovingly. A man or woman who will speak slightingly of a life companion has outraged the first principles of happiness in the marriage relation—respect and politeness—and is not fit to be trusted.

In this respect I am inclined to think that man suffers more than woman. For man is still essentially the hunter, the one who experiences the desires and thrills of the chase, and dreams ever of coming unawares upon Diana in the woodlands. . . . I think that, in the interests of husbands, an important piece of advice to wives is: Be always escaping . . . ensure that you allow your husband to come upon you only when there is delight in the meeting. Whenever the finances allow, the husband and wife should have separate bedrooms, failing that they should have a curtain which can at will be drawn so as to divide the room they share.

—*Married Love,* 1918 1872

REGARD ONE ANOTHER SELFLESSLY. The very nearest approach to domestic felicity on earth is in the mutual cultivation of an absolute unselfishness. Let each one strive to yield oftenest to the wishes of the other. Neglect the whole world besides, rather than one another. Never allow a request to be repeated; "I forgot" is never an acceptable excuse. Do not herald the sacrifices you make to each other's tastes, habits, or preferences. Let all your mutual accommodations be spontaneous, whole-souled, and free as air.

Matrimony and Finance

The husband should at the commencement of his married life tell his wife, as nearly as possible, the expected amount of his income; and together they should plan for its disbursement, in the most satisfactory manner to both.

A certain sum should be set aside for home expenses; rent, fuel, taxes, insurance, and all the minor details should be specified. The husband may take so much for his personal expenses and allow the wife a similar sum, also, setting aside a fund for contingent expenses.

When the items are all arranged with an eye to exactness (and accuracy is a cardinal virtue), the sum should be divided into monthly or weekly portions, and given regularly into the wife's hands; and the husband should not interfere with her department unless asked to do so.

If a man has married a decided simpleton or a spendthrift, he must make the best of his position, but if a woman of common discernment is thrown upon her own resources and given the purse, as well as the charge of household affairs, she rarely fails to develop good executive powers. The root of evil is in the failure on the part of the husbands to trust them, rather than on the part of the wives to execute their trust.

*—A Manual of Etiquette with Hints on
Politeness and Good Breeding, 1873*

Pet Him

Men, too, are at heart eternally children, and such tender petting as comforts children warms and sweetens a grown man's life. The "good night" should be a time of delightful forgetting of the outward scars of the years, and a warm, tender, perhaps playful exchange of confidences.

—*Married Love,* 1918

Chapter Five

For the Mother, as She Comforts and Cares for Them

Each wisely brought up and well-educated child is the best of all investments of a parent's wealth of money, affection, and effort.

Rules for Their Sleep

Provide separate sleeping enclosures. Where should the infant sleep? Never in bed between the parents. When placed between the parents, the infant must constantly inhale the poisonous emanations from the bodies of two adults. It should sleep by the side of the mother's bed in a crib.

Use proper bedding. The best bed at all seasons of the year is one of oat straw. This is light and soft. It is better than hair, because the straw can often be changed and the tick washed. In cold weather, a thick woolen blanket should be doubled and spread over the straw bed to increase the warmth. For covering the little sleeper, woolen blankets should alone be used.

At Night

SILENCE and night were in the air,
I heard their whispers everywhere;
And wind-breaths through the wall-flowers went
Like unseen bees in search of scent.
Deep in the sky some stars were burning,
And then—I heard the round world turning!

—*Enchanted Tulips and Other Verses for Children*, 1914

USE PROPER PILLOWS. The pillow as well as the bed should be of straw. The heads of American children are for the most part little furnaces! I have seen scores of babies die of brain maladies, who would have recovered if their brains had not been baked in feather pillows.

ATTEND THE CHILD AT BEDTIME. Give him light suppers and put him to bed early in a dark room. See that his feet are warm, his stomach easy, and his body not overloaded with blankets and quilts; also, see that the nursery is clean and freshly aired. He will not grow better in a glare of artificial light any more than will your camellias and azaleas.

MAKE CLOTHES FOR SLEEPING. Children should not wear the same garment next to the skin at night which they have worn through the day. If the nightgown is worn more than one night without going to the wash room, it should be hung up to be thoroughly aired during the day, if possible in the sun.

Pray with them. Pray with the child in simple and earnest language he can understand. The following beautiful little prayer is said to have been composed and used by a boy thirteen years old:

Father, now the day is past, on thy child thy blessing cast;
Near my pillow hand in hand, keep thy guardian angel band;
And throughout the darkling night, bless me with a cheerful light.
Let me rise at morn again, free from every care and pain;
Pressing through life's thorny way, keep me, Father, day by day.

—*The Ladies' Repository,* June 1865

Soothe the child who cannot sleep. Nervous children who toss and turn and cry out that they cannot go to sleep may sometimes be quieted by having their feet rubbed vigorously with a flesh brush. A warm bath will sometimes be effectual, but generally it does not conduce to quiet so much as waken. After adjusting the physical appliances which tend to sleep, tell him to picture himself a little winding brook off in the deep woods carrying upon it a leaf or a chip.

Let them wake of themselves. Never wake up young children of a morning; it is a barbarity.

Rules for Their Diets

The quality of food intended for little children should be carefully studied, as the firmness of their flesh and the hardness of their bones is so dependent upon it.

Let nutrition, variety, and time of year guide selections. Every care must be taken to supply children with a variety and abundance of nutritious and digestible food, in which fruit, the cereals, vegetables, milk, mutton, beef, and poultry should be included together with simple sweets and plain puddings chiefly composed of milk, eggs, and flour or bread.

Feed their hunger. When children get hungry more often than the occurrence of the regular family meals, they should be supplied with a light repast of digestible character. If a child is hungry, it cannot be well or happy.

Don't forget milk. Wherever milk is used plentifully, there the children grow into robust men and women; wherever the place is usurped by tea, we have degeneracy, swift and certain.

Serve their meals thus:

- The breakfast should be early and plentiful.
- Mid-day dinners should be varied and always hot—indeed, all food is most digestible when warm—and composed of some plain meat dish, at least two vegetables, and a simple pudding. Soup is invaluable for children, but it must be plain.
- The supper, given about two hours before retiring, should be light and nutritious and may include warm bread, any form of porridge and milk, custard, simple stewed fruits, and either cool water or cocoa.

Particular Rules for Feeding Little Ones under Three

These outlines will serve to guard those having the care of children from making the mistakes which too often entail a life of weakness or suffering as the consequence equally of injudicious indulgence and of neglect of the most ordinary rules of health.

Limit his fare. Grant him novel food sparingly and with discretion as to kind. His stomach is too delicate an organ to be tampered with. Let milk—scalded or boiled, as a rule—be the staple, mixed with farina, barley, or something of the sort. Let him munch Graham bread and light crackers freely. Remove far from him hot bread and griddle cakes.

Keep watch over the cooking. Unless you have a nurse whom you know for yourself to be faithful and experienced, always superintend the cooking of your baby's food.

SUPPLY PLENTY OF BREAD. Children who have cut all their teeth will thrive well and grow strong if they eat heartily of good bread every day. Homemade bread should be eaten in preference to baker's bread, because in baker's bread some of those valuable nutritive parts are destroyed, and while it satisfies hunger, it does not nourish the body.

GIVE TO HIM THESE FOODS:
- Mealy old potatoes—never new or waxy ones.
- Young onions, boiled in two waters.
- Fresh asparagus, green peas, and dry sweet potatoes should suffice for vegetables.
- Rice and hominy, of course.

GIVE HIM THESE, ONCE IN A WHILE, FOR DESSERT:
- A simple custard.
- A taste of homemade ice cream, rice, and farina puddings.
- Graham hasty pudding.
- The inner part of a well-roasted apple.
- In their season, ripe peaches.

MOTHER, PROTECT HIM. Hundreds of infants have been killed by parents in giving them improper foods; thus, take care to avoid:
- Food prepared for other members of the family, as the table foods may be poisonous to the infant.
- Skin of an apple, which is as bad for him as a bit of your kid gloves would be; and the skin of a grape, more indigestible than sole leather.
- Raisins—skins and all—which are unfit for anybody to eat and poisonous for a baby.

NEVER GIVE A CHILD UNDER TWO YEARS OF AGE THESE FOODS:
- Ham, bacon, or pork in any other form.
- Cabbage, pickles, or other succulent vegetables.

- Coffee, tea, beer, wine, cider, or any other alcoholic liquor of any kind.
- Bananas, berries, or other fruit except prune juice.
- Pastries or preserves.

Recipes for the Nursery

Some of the finest children I have seen were reared upon this diet:

CONDENSED MILK. This is perhaps the safest substitute for the "good milk from one cow," which few mothers in town can procure. Keep the can in a cool place and mix according to its directions.

FARINA. Stir 1 large tablespoon Hecker's Farina, wet up with cold water, into 1 cup boiling water (slightly salted) in the farina kettle (i.e, one boiler set within another, the latter filled with hot water). Boil 15 minutes, stirring constantly until it is well thickened. Then add 1 cup fresh milk, stirring in gradually, and boil 15 minutes longer. Sweeten with 2 teaspoons white sugar and give to the child as soon as it is cool enough. You may make enough in the morning to last all day; warming it up with a little hot milk as you want it. Keep it in a cold place, do not get it too sweet, and cook it well.

ARROWROOT. Stir arrowroot paste of 2 teaspoons best Bermuda arrowroot, wet with cold water, into 1 cup boiling

The Care of a Child

Nursing women should not give way to temper. Anger, anxiety, suspense, fear, terror, and undue conditions of any kind will turn the milk to poison.

Gradual weaning is much better than the sudden removal of the child from the breast.... A child should not be weaned in the hot months.

—*Sloan's Cook Book and Advice to Housekeepers*, 1905

water with one small pinch of salt; stir and boil 5 minutes or until it is clear; add 2 even teaspoons white sugar, dissolved in 1 cup fresh milk. Boil 10 minutes, slowly, still stirring. If the child has fever or cannot digest milk, substitute hot water for it.

Milk and bread. Crumble 2 tablespoons stale Graham bread into ½ cup boiled milk, sweeten with a very little sugar; when cool enough, feed to the child with a spoon.

Wheaten grits. Soak 4 tablespoons grits (cracked wheat) in a little cold water 1 hour and then put into the kettle. Boil the soaked grits in a quart of water 1 hour, stirring up often; add 1 cup milk and a pinch of salt and boil half an hour longer. Sweeten to taste and, if the child is well, pour cream over it. This is designed for children over a year old.

Graham hasty pudding. Stir 1 cup Graham flour, wet up with cold water, into 1 large cup boiling water with 1 teaspoon salt. Boil 10 minutes, stirring almost constantly. Add 1 large cup milk and cook, after it has come again to a boil, 10 minutes longer. Give with sugar and milk for breakfast. Eaten with cream, nutmeg, and powdered sugar, this is a good plain dessert for grown people as well as children.

Thoughts on Their Dress (And Yours)

Dress little girls warmly. On cold, windy days, I am pained to see the efforts of foolish parents to freeze their little girls. It is an outrage. The poor little shivering things are sent out into the streets with their heads comfortably protected and thick shawls around their shoulders, which comparatively need no protection, yet with their skirts standing out at an angle of 45 degrees and their poor little drum-stick legs as unprotected from the blasts as the legs of a turkey hanging in a meat stall.

Protect their arms and shoulders. If the mother desires to exhibit her darling's beautiful skin, let her cut out a bit of the dress upon its chest; when the neighbors come in, let her show the skin thus exposed to the company. This skin is so near the furnace of the body it has no chance to get cold; but, in the case of the arms and legs, the blood has to make a long journey before it can return to the chest for a new supply of warmth. These parts, therefore, need special protection. As cold currents of blood come from both arms back into the vital organs, they play the mischief there. To save a child from croup, pneumonia, and other grave affections, keep her arms warm.

DO NOT CONTRACT THE WAISTS OF YOUR LITTLE GIRLS. Thousands of women are rendered unfit for marriage and motherhood by what they suffer as the result of tight lacing. There are scores of corset-wearing mothers, but point out to me one healthy one out of each score, and I'll show you 19 prematurely wrinkled and wan, fretful, and ailing women to offset your one.

MIND YOUR OWN DRESS FOR THEM. Many a good, kind, loving mother has made her son or her daughter extremely unhappy by ap-

---

Mercerized cheviot, madras and the new silky-looking French ginghams are made into the most charming summer frocks for girls who are still wearing short skirts. White embroidery, straps and tabs of white linen or pique and even coarse laces are used for trimmings. A dainty little frock of pink and white French gingham has a large bertha of white pique. Another delightful costume is of pale-blue chambray, with a fancy bertha of tucked white lawn and lace.

White stockings are still considered the smart thing for little tots to wear with all sorts of light-colored costumes. Very odd these tiny white legs look coming out beneath the modish black silk coats.

—"Styles of the Month for Children," May 1908

The reason we admire the tapering waist is because we have been wrongly educated. We have acquired wrong ideas of beauty. We have accepted the ideals of the fashion-plate rather than those of the Creator. We find that some form of physical deformity maintains in almost every country. The Chinese deform the feet, and we think this is barbarous, but it is really not as serious as the deforming of the vital parts of the body.

—*What a Young Woman Ought to Know*, 1898

pearing not as well dressed, or not as considerate of the ways of the world as her children have a right to expect. We are told in the good book about respect due to our parents, but you and I and the other women have a duty to respect our children, and not to cause them to be mortified by our personal appearance. This may sound a little cruel, but I am sure you will see its truth if you will only remember the times when you have seen your boy's or your girl's face flush because "mother didn't look like the other ladies."

Some Advice for Their Playtime

AMUSE THE BABY SIMPLY:

- One mother used to give her baby a wide-mouthed bottle and a box of beans, and he would amuse himself for a long time dropping them one by one into the bottle.

- Another amusement for when he was just old enough to stand beside a chair was to give him a lead pencil and let him poke holes through a paper as it lay across a cane-seated chair. A simple device, but it helped the mother "make time," and so the end desired was gained.

LET THEM MAKE THEIR OWN PLAYTHINGS. A little girl had better fashion her cups and saucers of acorns than to have a set of earthen ones supplied. A boy takes ten times more pleasure in a little wooden cart he has pegged together than he would in a painted and gilded carriage bought from the toy shop.

MAKE HER A DOLL. For the wee girl, make a nice rag doll; it will please her as well as a bought one; besides, that sort of dollie can be handled ever so roughly without any danger of breaking its neck or limbs.

For a little lady of two-and-a-half years this will do:

She had picked up a cane in the corner of the room and was playing with it—a place stick bent at the end. Papa asked, "What are you doing with the cane?"

"It isn't a cane."

"What is it, then?"

"It's an umbrella without any clothes on."

—*Harper's New Monthly Magazine,* 1868

SEND THEM OUT. The truth is that "all out-doors," as the phrase is, is the only proper apartment for children. Nothing can make up for it—for the gleeful delight of picking shells upon the seashore, or paddling with dimpled feet in the foam of the waves, or plucking a handful of flowers wherever one chooses to stray, or looking at the animal creation, every one of which, from a caterpillar to an ox, is a marvel and wonder compared to which a toy shop is of no interest whatever. We are taking it for granted that such a child is neither fettered by fine clothes nor tyrannized over by a stupid, ignorant, selfish nurse.

TAKE YOUR BABY OUT, TOO. A baby can no more flourish in the dark than a flower. Like the flower, it needs sunshine, and should, like it, have the direct rays from the sun. Do not fear its eyes will be injured

Baby outdoors

if the sun shines on its face; and when you take it out to ride, unless the sun is very strong, do not cover up its face with the carriage top.

ENCOURAGE FRIENDSHIPS. Children, to be truly happy, must have the companionship of other children. Unless a child's companions are really objectionable, the evil of no companionship is greater than the risk of letting him play with his mates.

GARDEN WITH THEM. Give children a corner "all their own" and some seeds to put in it. Show them how to make beds and take care of them; tell them how flowers grow and encourage them to watch and study them. Such employment will keep them out of a great deal of mischief.

Threading a Needle

SURELY I think Nurse has forgotten
How hard it is to thread this cotton—
It is so very long ago
Since she was small like me and slow—
Thread, needle, thread, Nurse says I must do it—
Dear Nurse, indeed the cotton won't come through it!
      —*Enchanted Tulips and Other Verses for Children*, 1914

MAKE FUN IN NATURE. Hunting nuts in the real woods is a joy which children should taste more often than they usually do, for in these days of railroads and electric cars the woods are not so very far off, and once a year at least there should be a nutting party in every well-regulated family.

Miscellaneous Recipes for Discontented Babies

TO SOOTHE THE TEETHING BABY. For the sleeplessness, irritability, and discomfort which so often accompany teething, much can be done by the mother:

❧ A hot footbath will often have a soothing effect by relieving the congestion in the head and mouth. Mustard can be added with benefit.

❧ A good movement of the bowels, induced with castor oil, will relieve congestion in the gums.

❧ The mother's finger dipped in syrup of lettuce can be gently carried over the tender and inflamed gum and, now and then, by a little firmer pressure, may allow the point of the tooth to free its way.

❧ Make a dried-flour mixture by tying 1 cup of flour into a stout muslin bag and dropping it into cold water. Then set the bag and water

In Marshall

I remember, in the summer of 1858, sitting on the broad piazza in front of our home in Marshall, Texas, watching the great comet that hung in the heavens. I can see now the crêpe myrtle bushes with their rose-colored blossoms, flanking the steps; feel again the warm, languorous air of the summer night, heavy with the odor of white jasmine, and honeysuckle; and hear again the voices, long stilled, as we talked together of the comet and its portent.... When we looked at the blazing comet in that fair summer sky, a feeling of awe and mystery enveloped us.

—*A Southern Girl in '61*, 1905

[54]

Soothing syrups are poisons to babies. They contain opium. Opium kills babies. Don't dope your baby.

over the fire. Boil three hours steadily. Turn out the flour ball and dry it in the hot sun all day; or, if you need it at once, dry it in a moderate oven without shutting the door. To use it, grate 1 tablespoon for a cup of boiling milk and water (half and half). Wet up the flour with a very little cold water; stir in, and boil five minutes. Put in a little salt.

TO SOOTHE COLICKY BABIES. Paregoric, whiskey, brandy, or soothing syrup are improper remedies for colic. Drugging the baby into insensibility will not cure the cause of illness. Colic is often a symptom of another condition, so this condition must be ascertained and treated thus:

❋ For colic that may come from cold hands and feet, keep a flannel belly band on the baby in both summer and winter.

❋ Colic is often due to constipation, in which case an enema of warm water—with the addition of salt at the rate of a level teaspoon to the pint—is required, followed by 1 or 2 teaspoons of castor oil or other gentle laxative medicine.

Miscellaneous Recipes for Sick Children

TO PREVENT CROUP. Take two skeins of black sewing silk, braid them together so they will wear well, and tie the braid loosely around the neck so it is worn below the clothes out of sight; and the child will never have the croup while it is worn. Now, some will laugh at this and call it an old woman's notion, but as it costs but little and can do no harm, if you will only try it, you will save the little ones lots of misery and yourselves many a sleepless night.

To treat croup. The instant croupy threatenings are observed, keep the child indoors and serve light food—and not much of that—until the symptoms have abated. Put a mustard plaster on the windpipe, and let it redden the skin but not blister. Put the child's feet in mustard water as hot as they can bear it. Then wipe them dry and keep them covered. Croup requires very prompt treatment; if home treatment does not relieve the child, send immediately for a physician.

To remedy a cough or whooping cough:

- Spread butter plentifully on paper (to protect clothing) and lay it over the chest, letting it come well up to the throat.
- Administer a syrup formed from sugar and onion juice.
- Rub the feet thoroughly with hog's lard before the fire, on

Whooping Cough Syrup

Make a syrup of prickly pear, a species of cactus, and drink freely. Take about three moderate sized leaves of the prickly pear to a quart of cold water, cut up in pieces and boil slowly about half an hour, strain out all the prickles through close muslin or linen, sweeten with white sugar and boil a little longer. A safe and sure cure, and so pleasant to the taste that infants will take it with a relish. It is also good for a cold that settles in the throat or lungs. This species of cactus grows in rocky and sandy places and is grown in gardens. I should say from a teaspoon to a tablespoon for a child, as needed, according to age. For an adult, one to two tablespoons.

—*Dr. Chase's Third Last and Complete Receipt Book and Household Physician,* 1903 going to bed—and keep the child warm therein.

- Rub the back, at lying down, with old rum; it seldom fails.
- Give a spoonful of juice of pennyroyal mixed with brown sugar candy twice a day.
- Give ½ pint of milk, warm from the cow, with the quantity of a nutmeg of conserve of roses dissolved in it, every morning.
- In desperate cases, change of air will have a good effect.

TO RELIEVE A TOOTHACHE. Cut a large raisin open, roast it or heat it, and apply it around the tooth while it is as hot as can be borne. It will operate like a little poultice and will draw out the inflammation.

Treatment of Jaundice in Children

J. E. Ball, M. D. of Texas reports a case which was printed in the April number of The Brief, as follows:

February 3rd: Called to a child 18 months old; skin and eyes as yellow as saffron, urine thick—stained its clothes that saffron color peculiar to jaundiced urine. Prescribed: Leptandrin, 1 gram; podophyllin, 1/2 gram; pulverized Jamaica ginger, 2 grams; mixed, and divided into 8 powders. Gave 1 powder every 4 hours until the biliary secretions were aroused. Also Tincture of buchu and sweet spirits of niter, each 1 dram, 10 drops every 2 hours.

February 5th: First prescriptions acted well. Then prescribed: Extract of fringe tree and tincture of blood root, each equal parts, 10 drops 4 times per day.

February 12th: Little patient entirely relieved; skin and urine as clear as it ever was.

—*Dr. Chase's Third Last and Complete*
Receipt Book and Household Physician, 1903

TO PREVENT RICKETS, TENDERNESS, AND WEAKNESS. Dip children in cold water every morning, at least till they are eight or nine months old. No roller should ever be put round their bodies, nor any stays used. Instead, when they are put into short petticoats, put a waistcoat under their frocks. It is best to wean a child when seven months old, if it be disposed to rickets. It should lie in the cradle at least a year.

Cures the Orphans

The Rev. Mother of the Convent of the Holy Family, Baltic, Conn., writes that she can speak very highly of the Kickapoo Indian Remedies. She always has a supply of each kind on hand the year around. For several years they have stood the test in every case. The health of the two hundred children under her care is paramount to everything else. A fever, cold or a cough is seldom known, thanks to the Kickapoo Indian Sagwa, Indian Oil, and Indian Cough Cure, while the Kickapoo Indian Salve and Kickapoo Indian Worm Killer have often proved their effectiveness as well.

—*Healy & Bigelow's New Cook Book,* 1890.

Chapter Six

For the Mother, as Instructress

The Parental Example

If parents realized how great is their responsibility, how closely they are watched and copied, they would place a perpetual guard upon their lips and manners.

Be what you would have them become. Mother, be what the children ought to be. Do what the children ought to do. Avoid what they should avoid. Know that those by whom you are surrounded are often only reflections of yourself. Are any among them defective? Examine what you are yourself, what you do, what you avoid—in a word, your whole conduct. Do you discover in yourself defects, sins, wandering? Begin by improving yourself and seek afterward to improve your children.

Assure that your husband is with them. The father who plunges into business so deeply that he has no leisure for domestic pleasures and whose only intercourse with his children consists in a brief word of authority or a surly lamentation over their intolerable expensiveness is to be both pitied and blamed.

BE HONEST, BE RIGHT. Let there be no deception, no trickery for the keen eye of childhood to detect. Rule your own spirit and wear an unruffled brow, lest the smiling cherub on your knee catch your angry frown. Never stoop to pander with expediency. If a question of right or wrong comes up for decision, meet it squarely. Let your children feel that mother and father are always found on the side of the right.

The Proper Use of Praise and Punishment

There are two great motives influencing human action—hope and fear. Both of these are at times necessary. But who would not prefer to have her child influenced to good conduct by a desire of pleasing rather than by the fear of offending?

UNDERSTAND AND REASON WITH THEM. The fear of ridicule, pain, and shame drives children into falsehoods. Lies caused by dread of punishment may be avoided if it is understood that a child guilty of a wrong should be forgiven if he made a straightforward, honest acknowledgment of the same. Children are very delicate instruments. Men play upon them as if they were tough as drums and, like drums, made for beating. Do not terrorize them, but reason gently and plainly with them. One in sympathy with their little souls will lead them along safely amid temptations to falsehood.

PRAISE THEM. Parents who never have a word of praise for their children, who deny a bit of approval or a welcoming smile to their own—although they are generous enough with both to strangers—do not know what they are doing. They are chilling the warmest feelings of the heart. They are withering the bright blossoms of love and confidence which cannot live without careful nurture.

PUNISH CONSISTENTLY. Let your punishments be consistent, direct, unhesitating, and not to be escaped; the punishment need not and should not be severe, just enough to let the sensitive heart of the child understand that mother is displeased. I think you will find that, by this

> *Helen* the eldest daughter, has just come home from school. She is the special, tender delight of her father's eye—pale and delicate in face and physique, clear blue eyes, and auburn hair.... At the sound of the dinner-bell, she slipped quietly into her accustomed place at table, unnoticed by her father, who was not in the secret of her arrival. Soon, in helping round, he came in course to Helen's plate, when he looked up, and lo! such a quick embrace of father and daughter! It was a picture, which only those who have had and have lost such fathers know how to appreciate.
>
> —"Aunt Sally's Home," February 1873

method, you reduce the punishment you would otherwise be compelled to inflict, for you soon secure a habit of obedience, after which punishments will be almost unnecessary.

ADMINISTER PUNISHMENT WITH SELF-POSSESSION. If done in a towering passion, punishment takes the character of revenge, and the child resists it with defiance, stubbornness, or a feeling of being the injured party. Place clearly before the child the nature of the aggravation and assure the child that the sole design of the chastisement is his present and future welfare.

PUNISH PRIVATELY. Never correct a child by scolding, admonition, or castigation in public. It is an attack on the child's self esteem, which provokes resistance and arouses a rebellious spirit which often breaks out in open defiance or sullen resentment.

REFRAIN FROM FAULT-FINDING. Scolding, finding fault, and recrimination are below the dignity of punishment. Nothing will rasp and embitter the soul more deeply than a railing, "nagging" tongue. Mothers often fall into the habit of chiding their children for every little offense. It is "Don't do this and don't do that," from morning until night. The command becomes odious to the child, and he pays as little attention to his mother's remonstrance as to a cat's meow.

Speak gently. I know some houses in which sharp, angry tones resound from morning till night, and the influence is as contagious as measles and much more to be dreaded in a household. The children catch it and it lasts for life—an incurable disease.

What to Teach at Home

There are few who can receive the honors of a college, but all are graduates of the hearth.

Cultivate their mental powers. Parents have been warned of late that a child with a precocious brain is more liable to dangerous diseases of the brain than other children and that indulging their precocious appetites will increase the excitement of the brain and result in inflammation and premature death. Parents have, therefore, been urged to retard the education of the mental powers, but modern mental science acknowledges that we may begin at a very early period to work upon the conceptive and perceptive faculties, not only without danger, but with manifest advantage.

Allow them choice of their own occupations. Watch the bent of the young minds; converse with them as to their predilections. They will learn any business more readily if they are interested in it. Let this determine you to leave them unfettered in their choice.

Teach them independence. All children should cherish a desire to do all they can for themselves and to support themselves by their labor as early as possible. Those who lean on father and mother for everything will find it hard work to get along by and by, as they may have to do when their parents die. Those who early learn to rely upon themselves will have little difficulty in earning their own living.

The Alphabet

LONG is the Alphabet
In my blue reading book:
There is each letter set,
With its peculiar look—
Some seeming fat and glad,
Others a little sad.

Some seeming very wise,
Some with a roguish look,
Making all kinds of eyes
In my blue reading book!
While a few seem to say,
"Shall you know us to-day?"

—*Enchanted Tulips and Other Verses for Children*, 1914

TEACH DAUGHTERS THE LESSONS OF THE HOME. No matter your daughter's position in her father's home, in our country of variable fortunes there is no insurance against her compulsion to go into the kitchen for her daily bread once she is a wife. The time may not come when the daughters of wealth shall be obliged to take their stand in the kitchen, but should they not know how to bake and wash? We shall never have good puddings and pies, chowders and fricassees, while the ladies are taught that it is a disgrace to learn to cook. Teach them how to make bread as well as rick-rack. If they show a talent for music, give them a chance, but not before they can broil a steak or make a decent cup of coffee.

TEACH SONS TO EARN THEIR OWN. Many an unwise parent labors hard and lives sparingly for the purpose of giving his children a start in the world, as it is called. Instead of striving to lay up fortunes for your son, teach him the habits of business and so give him treasures more staple than stocks and bonds. Setting a young man afloat with money left by relatives is like tying bladders under the arms of one who cannot swim; ten chances to one he will lose his bladders and go to the bottom. Teach him to swim.

Rules for Children's Deportment

It is the practice with certain people to sneer at the word "etiquette" and to claim it merely means a foolish pandering to frivolous customs which in themselves have no meaning or use. This is a misapprehension which a little thoughtful consideration will remove. A knowledge of etiquette may be said to be an important part of good breeding.

RESPECT FOR OTHERS. Children can be trained to reciprocate courtesies and to behave politely everywhere without making prim little martinets of them. Teach them to respect each other's rights—to enjoy their merry romp and innocent fun without hurting each other's feelings or playing upon some weakness.

OBEDIENCE. The first lesson a child should be taught is filial respect and a deferent yielding of its own wishes to those of its parents. This does not imply a slavish submission or a crushing-out of individuality. It means that the tie between parent and child should be so strong and the confidence so great that there would be no chance for the clashing of will.

COURTESY. Children must not be allowed to have two sets of manners, one for home and one for company. They can be taught to exercise gentle manners at home, to be thoughtful of the comfort of every family member, and to be guilty of no act that they would blush for were other eyes upon them. Then they will become real gentlemen or ladies.

Respect for Elders. Teach them to be deferent to their superiors in age and position. "Young America" has the idea that it is a proof of independence to speak flippantly and sneeringly of parents or guardians, referring to them as "the governor," "the old lady," or "the old party." There is no greater mistake made, and the listeners who may smile at such "wit" will just as likely censure for such coarseness and disrespect.

Fairness. Teach them to be fair in play and not to cheat. This may be a hard lesson to learn, but it is one of the grandest.

Silence. It is very rude for children to ask direct questions, such as "Where are you going?" or "What have you got in that package?" In fact, they should not show curiosity about other people's affairs.

Modesty. Modesty among boys and girls is as highly appreciated as among grown people; and a young person who thinks himself a little better than his associates can hardly help carrying the thought into action. By such conduct he makes himself exceedingly disagreeable.

Manners. Many children form habits which are not nice, such as spitting on the floor, scratching the head, stretching themselves out upon a chair, and yawning. All such habits are exceedingly low bred.

Succinctness. If they have occasion to enter a place of business, train your children to state what they want and then retire as quickly as possible. They have no right to encroach upon the time of a businessman.

Teaching Table Manners

Some little folks are not polite at their meals. The following standards are so simple . . . we take pleasure in placing them conspicuously before our readers. They will bear memorizing.

In silence I must take my seat;
And give God thanks before I eat;
Must for my food in patience wait
Till I am asked to hand my plate;
I must not scold, nor whine, nor pout,
Nor move my chair or plate about;
With knife, or fork, or napkin ring,
I must not play—nor must I sing;
I must not speak a useless word;
For children must be seen—not heard;
I must not talk about my food,
Nor fret if I don't think it good;
My mouth, with food I must not crowd,
Nor while I'm eating speak aloud;
Must turn my head to cough or sneeze,
And when I ask, say, "If you please;"
The tablecloth I must not spoil,
Nor with my food my fingers soil;
I must keep my seat when I am done,
Nor round the table sport or run;
When told to rise, then I must put
My chair away with noiseless foot,
And lift my heart to God above,
In praise for all his wondrous love.

—*The Ladies' Repository*, 1865

Chapter Seven

For the Nurse

Keep up a fire. The sight of a bright blaze is calculated to cheer the patient, while the sight of a dark, closed stove is depressing. By no means allow a sick person to be in a room warmed by a flue or register.

Keep him cheered. The patient should be indulged in every fancy that is not hurtful. Study all pleasant and soothing arts to while away the time and keep worry of every kind away from him. A trifle at which you can laugh will be a burden to the enfeebled mind and body of a patient who has nothing to do but lie still and roll it over in his mind until it swells into a mountain.

Welcome the sun for him. Cases are not rare in which invalids have been restored to health by using sunbaths and otherwise freely enjoying the sunshine. The old idea of darkening the sick room is exploded. The modern science of physics has come to recognize sunshine as one of the most powerful of remedial agencies. If the patient's eyes are weak, admit the sunshine from a quarter where it will not fall upon them.

CLEAN WHILE THE PATIENT IS OUT. Let such sweeping and dusting as are necessary be also done with dispatch, using a dust-pan to receive the dust from the carpet. Avoid raising clouds of dust from the carpet, and of ashes from the fireplace. Make arrangements for the patient on returning from a convalescent drive to find the room thoroughly cleaned, aired, and adorned with fresh flowers (always so cheering in a sick room), and let the bed be nicely made up and turned down.

MANAGE ODORS. It is best to have no odors in the sick room unless it be bay rum, German cologne, or something else especially fancied by the sick person. Cologne water will not dispel a foul odor, while disinfectants are noisome. When there is any unpleasant exhalation, it is far better to let is escape by properly ventilating the room than to try to overcome it by the aid of perfumery. In fevers, where there are offensive exhalations from the body, sponging the patient with tepid water will help remove the odor.

MIND HIS SENSITIVITIES. Do not keep the medicines where he can see them, nor ever let him witness the mixing of that which he is to swallow. As soon as his meals are over, remove every vestige of them

---

And even while she talked, she had propped me up comfortably and was passing her cool fingers over my burning head. Gay and thoughtless as she was, all her selfishness, and all her frivolity, seemed to be left outside the threshold. In the sick-room she was nothing but tenderness and self-forgetfulness.

"There, aunty," she said, when she had arranged me to her satisfaction, "you never looked so pretty in your life. The fever has just given color enough to your cheeks, and your eyes sparkle like diamonds. I declare, you're quite a beauty."

—"The Two Lovers,"
March 1871

> "*I* should not say that Miss Hartley looked like a well woman," replied Dr. Houghton, as, coming forward, he looked earnestly and very kindly in my face; and then, taking the seat placed for him, he softly lifted my hand from the counterpane and held it in his own, as he continued: "I feared this—and now we must see what can be done for you; I wish I could have seen you last night, but it is better now than later. Do you know what a lovely evening you are losing by being shut up here, and will you allow me to put back the curtain a little that you may see the sunset?"
>
> —"The Two Lovers," March 1871

from the room. Even a soiled spoon, lying on table or bureau, may offend his fastidious appetite. Cover the stand or waiter from which he eats with a spotless napkin, and serve his food in your daintiest ware.

ARRANGE A DRIVE. Driving is a delightful recreation for convalescents; they should be indulged in it as soon as the physician pronounces it safe. In winter, they should be carried driving about noon so as to enjoy the sunshine at its warmest. In summer, the cool of the morning or evening is the best time to drive them out, but, if the latter time be chosen, be careful to return immediately after sundown. It is well to have some little refreshment awaiting the patient after a drive—a little cream or milk toddy, a cup of tea or coffee, or, if the weather be hot, some cooling draught perhaps would be more acceptable.

DO NOT ADMIT VISITORS. In a case of illness, many well-meaning persons crowd to see the patient. Do not admit them into the sick room, as it is too exciting and fatiguing to an ill person to see company; and, when in a critical condition, the balance might be disastrously turned by the injudicious admission of visitors.

Texas for Invalids or Consumptives

While there is no way known to remedy mortality, yet a large share of it is avoidable. This remedy consists in a change of climate. For some years I have given this matter considerable attention, and am satisfied that there is no locality in the United States, and perhaps not on the western hemisphere, equal to the highlands of central and southwestern Texas. The climate there is dry, mild and salubrious. The elevation takes one above the damps and fog which are so fatal in Florida and on the sea coasts generally.

As to the best place to go in Texas, A. G. Hayson, M.D., of Minden, La., in Medical Brief, '83, says to the editor: "Eighty miles west of San Antonio, Tex., is found a beautiful valley lying in the gap of the mountains, with an average width of 4 miles by 18 long. This valley, or 'Sabinal Canyon,' as it is called there, has gushing mountain springs and bright, clear running streams that never go dry. I met there, in 1875, two gentlemen who had, previous to going there, pulmonary hemorrhage. Both seemed to be in perfect health, and so expressed themselves. This canyon, with its pure-aired atmosphere, its mountain scenery, with beautiful stretches of prairie and timber, and here and there, standing alone in the distance, knots of live oak and pecan, make it one of the most beautiful as well as romantic places I have ever seen. I do not think a better place for consumptives can be found."

—*Dr. Chase's Third Last and Complete Receipt Book and Household Physician*, 1903

Miscellaneous Recipes for Ailing Adults

TO REMEDY ALMOST ANYTHING. Break an egg. Separate the yolk and white. Whip each to a stiff froth. Add 1 tablespoon of arrowroot and a little water to the yolk. Rub till smooth and free from lumps.

Pour slowly into a ½ pint of boiling water, stirring all the time. Let it simmer till jelly-like. Sweeten to the taste and add 1 tablespoon of French brandy. Stir in the frothed white and take hot in winter. In summer, set first on ice, then stir in the beaten white. Milk may be used instead of water.

TO CURE THE HEART OF AN ACHE. Take a piece of the lean of mutton, about the size of a large walnut, put it into the fire and burn it for some time, till it becomes almost reduced to a cinder, then put it into a clean rag and squeeze it until some moisture is expressed, which must be dropped in the ear as hot as the patient can bear.

Professor Gunn's Treatment for Burns from Gunpowder

In burns from gunpowder, where the powder has been deeply imbedded in the skin, a large poultice made of common molasses and wheat flour, applied over the burnt surface, is the very best thing that can be used, as it seems to draw the powder to the surface, and keep the injured part so soft that the formation of scars does not occur. It should be removed twice a day, and the part washed with a shaving brush and warm water before applying the fresh poultice. The poultice should be made sufficiently soft to admit of its being readily spread on a piece of cotton. In cases in which the skin and muscles have been completely filled with the burnt powder, we have seen the parts heal perfectly, without leaving the slightest mark to indicate the position or nature of the injury.

—*Dr. Chase's Third Last and Complete Receipt Book and Household Physician*, 1903

To treat acute cardiac pain. Whether or not the pain is due to angina pectoris, a mustard plaster will relieve you.

To cure those addicted to drinking wine. Put in a sufficient quantity of wine 3 or 4 large eels, and leave there till quite dead. Give that wine to the person you want to reform, and he or she will be so much disgusted with wine, that though they formerly made use of it, they will now have an aversion to it.

To bind a cut. Dissolve ocean salt in a pitcher of water and rub this on the flesh with a sponge; or apply cobwebs and brown sugar or the dust of tea, applied with laudanum.

To treat a burn or scald. Cover it with wet linen cloths, pouring on more water without removing them till the pain is alleviated, when pure hog's lard may be applied. Or apply lather of soap from the shaving cup with the brush to produce relief. White of egg applied in the same way is also a simple and useful dressing. If the shock is great and there is no reaction, administer frequently aromatic of ammonia or a little brandy and water till the patient rallies.

To treat venomous bites. Apply a moderately tight ligature above the bite. Wash the wound freely with water to encourage bleeding, then cauterize thoroughly. Afterwards, apply lint dipped in equal parts of olive oil and spirits hartshorn; swallow 10 drops dissolved in a wineglass of water.

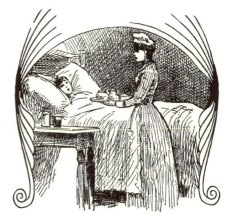

TO CURE A TOOTHACHE. Saturate a piece of wool with a mixture of 6 grains morphia and a ½ ounce each of tincture of aconite root, chloroform, laudrum, creosote, oil cloves, and cajuput; add as much gum camphor as the chloroform will dissolve. Put it in the hollow tooth, being certain that the cavity is cleaned out. Catnip leaves are also reputed beneficial for a toothache when masticated and applied to the decayed tooth.

To the People of Austin: Save Twenty Per Cent.

Austin, Texas, Sept. 11th, 1899.

From and after this date we have decided to adopt the Cash System. Believing as we do that the man who pays cash for his goods is entitled to buy them cheaper than the man who buys his goods on credit. Now as an inducement to cash purchasers to deal with us, we have decided to give a 20 Per Cent Rebate from all regular prices. . . .

1. The coupons will always be accepted by us as 5 cents (in half payments) for everything in our store except Stamps, Cigarettes, Chewing and Smoking Tobacco.

2. The coupon is given free with each retail 25 cent sale of Drugs, Prescriptions, Patent Medicine, Perfumery, Toilet Articles, Rubber Goods, Soda Water, Whiskies, Wines, and Brandies for medicinal purposes.

TOBIN DRUG CO.

—Advertisement in *The Capitol Cook Book*, 1899

To cure a headache. The fresh juice of ground ivy snuffed up the nose; ginger powder, formed into a plaster with warm water and applied on paper or cloth to the forehead; a mustard poultice applied to the nape of the neck; or a footbath, taken for the purpose of drawing the blood from the head, can all relieve aching of the head.

To relieve testicular pain. The constant use of an elm bark poultice, regularly changed every four hours, will be found a superior remedy for the excruciating pains of the testes which accompany the metastasis of mumps, whether of recent or long standing.

To allay nausea. Cloves may be used to allay vomiting and sickness at stomach, to stimulate the digestive functions, improve the flavor or operation of other remedies, and prevent a tendency toward digestion producing sickness or griping.

To relieve dysentery. Steep black or green tea in boiling water and sweeten with loaf sugar.

To relieve constipation. Castor oil is frequently used to remove constipation. One part oil of turpentine mixed with 3 or 4 parts castor oil increases its purgative effect. The greatest objections to this cathartic are its nauseous taste and tendency to cause sickness or unconquerable disgust. This may be overcome by adding to 1 pint of the oil 1 ounce of sassafras oil; the dose of this may be given in sweetened water. Any other aromatic oils will answer equally as well. When not contraindicated, the oil may be taken in wine, spirituous liquors, or the froth of beer, likewise in cinnamon or peppermint water.

To prevent dyspepsia. In most countries, people who indulge in alcoholic drinks take them at meal times or immediately after eating, when the membranous lining of the stomach is in some degree protected from their inflammatory action by a poultice, so to speak, of masticated food. The American imbiber prefers to swallow liquid poison when there is nothing in the organ into which he decants it to qualify its fiery principle or prevent it from taking immediate and full effect upon the viscera with which it comes in contact. Is it any wonder, then, considering the outrages the people of this country commit upon their internal machinery, that dyspepsia is a "national disease"? Take alcohol with your food and not alone.

Pleasant to Take

Messrs. C.I. Hood & Co.:

Last fall my boy had a humor develop itself around his finger nails which would fester up, become very sore, and cause the to nail come off; finally it left his fingers and went to his nose, first inside, and at last reaching down on the outside of the nostril, near the lip. We used various remedies without benefit. His general health became very much impaired. I went to my family physician (Dr. Green), and he ordered sarsaparilla. I got a bottle of your make (Hood's Sarsaparilla), and in five or six weeks the humor began to heal and continued to steadily till entirely well, and his sickly, puny look changed to one of vigor and health. He has taken it most of the time since, as I am desirous of eradicating this humor entirely from his blood. It is exceedingly commendatory of your Sarsparilla that it is so pleasant to take that he really likes it and will call for it.

> Very truly yours,
> John G. Rogers,
> (Firm of Stiles, Rogers, & Co.)
> Market Street, Lowell, Mass.

—Hood's Cook Book Reprint Number One, post 1877

To remedy dyspepsia:

Before breakfast. Rise early, dress warm, and go out. If strong, walk; if weak, saunter. After half an hour or more, come in for breakfast. Drink cold water three times. Of all cold baths, a morning bath is best for the dyspeptic.

Breakfast. For breakfast, eat a piece of good steak half as large as your hand, a slice of coarse bread, and a baked apple; eat very slowly. Avoid hot biscuits and strong coffee, and drink nothing. Talk very pleasantly with your neighbors; read cheerful comments of journals.

Work out of doors. Digest for an hour, and then to your work; I trust it is in the open air. Work hard till noon, and then rest body and mind till dinner; sleep a little and drink water.

Dinner. For dinner at two or three o'clock, eat a slice of beef, mutton, or fish as large as your hand, a potato, two or three spoons of other vegetables, and a slice of coarse bread; give more than half an hour to this meal, and use no drink.

After dinner. After dinner, play anaconda poker for an hour.

The Tongue—What It Tells

If ever I was so far left to myself as to meditate some rash act, I should first have a look at my tongue. If it was not perfectly clean and moist I should not consider myself perfectly healthy, nor perfectly sane, and would postpone my proceedings in the hope that my worldly prospects would get brighter. The tongue sympathizes with every trifling ailment of body or mind, and more especially with the state of the stomach. I sincerely believe that real comfort cannot be secured in this world by any one who does not keep his feet warm, his head cool, and his tongue clean.

—Dr. Chase's *Third Last and Complete Receipt Book and Household Physician*, 1903

Doctor Sangrado held that all human diseases should be cured by letting blood. Let a man travel six weeks in western Texas; and if he is not cured by its brambly phlebotomy of whatever ailment he has, it will be because there is no blood left in him. Of the thirteen kinds of bushes I counted—to say nothing of the sixty odd varieties of cactus—there is only one important exception which does not seem to have been created solely to make people healthy; and that one exception, the clieriondia, reeks with the combined potency of garlic and asafetida. But these thorns hatchel the air of western Texas wonderfully clean and blue.

—"Solid Days in Texas,"
June 1871

Supper. Forgo it. Even a little tea and toast will slow your recovery.

Bedtime routine. In a warm room, bathe your skin with cold water hastily; go to bed in a well-ventilated room before nine o'clock. Follow this prescription for three months, and your stomach will so far recover that you can indulge for some time in all sorts of irregular and gluttonous eating. Or if you have resolved, in the fear of Heaven, to present your body a living sacrifice, holy and acceptable unto God, then continue to eat and work like a Christian, and your distressing malady will soon be forgotten.

TO RELIEVE COUGHS. Boil 1 ounce licorice root in a ½ pint of water till it is reduced by half. Then add 1 ounce gum arabic and 1 ounce loaf sugar. Take 1 teaspoon every few hours. Or, boil 3 lemons for 15 minutes. Slice them thin while hot over 1 pound of loaf sugar. Put on the fire in a porcelain-lined saucepan and stew till the syrup is quite thick. After taking it from the fire, add 1 tablespoon oil of sweet almonds. Stir till thoroughly mixed and cool. Take one spoonful or more when the cough is troublesome. If more than a small quantity is desired, double the above proportions.

TO PREVENT COLDS. When I go to the house of a friend in the country and unexpectedly remain for the night, having no nightcap, I should naturally catch cold. But by tying a bit of pack-thread tightly round my head, I go to sleep imagining that I have a nightcap on, and consequently I catch no cold at all.

Many a cold, cough, and consumption are excited into action by pulling off the hat and overcoat by men, and bonnet and shawl by women, immediately on entering the house in winter after a walk. An interval of at least five or ten minutes should be allowed.

Insert feet in a mustard bath of 3 or 4 tablespoons powdered mustard to a hot footbath, removing when the skin reddens and begins to smart. This is also useful in the early stages of colds to induce perspiration.

Other Conditions and Cures

Other substances with the ability to heal various conditions:

Ginger is eminently useful in habitual flatulency, atonic dyspepsia, hysteria, and enfeebled and relaxed habits, especially of old and gouty individuals. Ginger, in the form of "ginger tea," is also popular and efficient in relieving the pangs of disordered menstruation.

The power of *lemonade* in preventing and arresting scurvy is unequaled by any other remedy, except a liberal supply of fresh vegetables of the cruciform family. Lemonade may be used freely and advantageously in the febrile and inflammatory diseases which produce reddened mucous membranes.

Ivy leaves in the form of decoction applied locally have been efficient in treating diseases of the skin, indolent ulcers, eczemas, and itch; this will also destroy vermin in the hair, which, it should be stated, is stained black by the application.

Parsley seeds, as well as the leaves, sprinkled on the hair in powder or in the form of an ointment, will destroy vermin.

Misteltoe is asserted to be of some value in restraining postpartum hemorrhages. It has also been beneficially employed in epilepsy, hysteria, insanity, paralysis, and other nervous diseases. In using this agent, it is always necessary to regulate the condition of the stomach and bowels, the menstrual discharge and other faulty secretions, and remove worms, if any are present, previous to its exhibition.

Sage is a valuable anaphrodisiac to check excessive venereal desires. It may be used in connection with moral, hygienic, and other aids, if necessary.

Vanilla is an aromatic stimulant said to exhilarate the brain, prevent sleep, increase muscular energy, and stimulate the sexual propensities. It is also considered an aphrodisiac, powerfully exciting the generative system and much used in perfumery and to flavor tinctures, syrups, ointments, and confectionery.

Mashed, raw onions applied to the soles of the feet will break up an ache-all-over cold, bid fever depart, and often effect a complete cure in a few hours. Family physicians have reported cases of typhoid fever, typhoid pneumonia, scarlet fever, and diphtheria cured by the use of this poultice unless the patient is very near death.

The juice of the *orange* has a direct beneficial medicinal influence in all fevers.

Nutmeg is also recommended for the cure of fever. Char a nutmeg by holding it to the flame and permitting it to burn by itself without disturbance; when charred, pulverize it, combine it with an equal quantity of burnt alum, and divide the mixture into three powders. On the commencement of the chill, give a powder. If this does not break it, give the second powder on the approach of the next chill; and if not cured, the third powder must be given as the succeeding chill comes on. Usually the first powder effects a cure.

Passionflower is especially useful to allay restlessness and overcome wakefulness when these are the result of exhaustion or the nervous excitement of debility. It proves especially useful in the insomnia of infants and old people. The sleep induced by passiflora, as it is known, is a peaceful, restful slumber, and the patient awakens quiet and refreshed.

Miscelleanous Recipes Just for Females

Preparation for Childbirth

The preparation of the bed is a matter of considerable importance and ought to be attended to during the early part of labor. Women usually deliver lying on the left side, with the knees drawn up towards the abdomen. The right side of the bed, therefore, is the one which requires preparing, and that part of it near the foot is preferable because the upper part of the bed is thus kept clean and comfortable for the patient when the labor is over, and because of the help derived from being able to plant the feet firmly against the bed-post during the pains.

☞ Two pillows are to be put in the center of the bed, so that the patient may lie with the upper part of the body directly across the bed, the hips being as near the edge as possible.

☞ As labor advances and it becomes necessary for the patient to be placed in bed, she should put on a clean chemise and night-dress. Amongst the working classes it is still too much the custom for women to be confined in their every-day dress. It is a practice that ought always to be discountenanced.

☞ The hair should be dressed in such a way that the continuous lying in bed after the confinement will not drag upon or entangle it more than is inevitable.

☞ It is very undesirable for a woman in labor to be surrounded by a number of friends and neighbors.

☞ No nurse should ever allow herself to be teased into prophesying that the labor will be over by a certain hour. If such prophesies turn out incorrect, as they are most likely to do, the patient loses courage and confidence.

☞ All gossip is to be avoided, and nurses should be particularly careful to make no reference to their past experiences, especially such as have been unfavorable. A good, kind nurse will not be at a loss for a few helpful and encouraging words as labor goes on and will not need to have recourse either to foolish promises or dismal anecdotes.

—*Dr. Chase's Third Last and Complete
Receipt Book and Household Physician*, 1903

TO FACILITATE CHILDBIRTH. Some physicians consider drinking a ½ pint of elm bark powder boiled in 1 pint of new milk daily, during and after the seventh month of gestation, as advantageous in facilitating and causing an easy delivery.

TO CURE CHAPS IN WOMEN'S NIPPLES. Apply balsam of sugar. Or, apply butter of wax, which speedily heals them.

TO SOFTEN HARD BREASTS. Apply turnips, roasted till soft then mashed and mixed with a little oil of roses. Change this twice a day, keeping the breast very warm with flannel.

TO RELIEVE SORE AND SWELLED BREASTS. Boil a handful of chamomile, and as much mallows in milk and water. Foment with it between two flannels, as hot as can be borne, every 12 hours. It also dissolves any knot or swelling in any part where there is no inflammation.

Abortion May Be Caused By

☞ External violence, such as kicks and blows or a fall, or violent action, such as dancing, riding, or jumping. Women in the state of pregnancy should avoid many of the domestic operations so proper at other times for good housewives to engage in. We venture, at the risk of exciting a smile, to mention some exertions that ought to be avoided, viz., hanging up curtains, bedmaking, washing, pushing in a drawer with the foot, careless walking up or down a stair.

- Straining of the body, as from coughing.

- Costiveness.

- Irritation of the neighboring parts, as from severe purging, falling down of the gut, or piles.

- Any sudden or strong emotion of the mind, such as fear, joy, or surprise.

- The pulling of a tooth; though toothache is occasionally very troublesome to women in the pregnant state, the operation of drawing teeth should, if possible, be avoided at that time.

- Marrying when rather advanced in age. It would be hazardous to name any particular age at which it is too late to marry, but the general observation is worth attending to.

- Constitutional debility from large evacuations, such as bleeding or purging, or from disease such as dropsy, fever, or smallpox.

- A robust and vigorous habit with great fullness of blood and activity of the vascular system.

- The death of the child.

—*Dr. Chase's Third Last and Complete Receipt Book and Household Physician*, 1903

Chapter Eight

For the Homemaker Setting Up Household

Furnishing and Decorating the Home

The greatest part of one's life is spent indoors, and the surroundings and decor of our particular abode tend to make our existence either more pleasant or unpleasant, either sober or mirthful in countenance.

Housekeeper's Alphabet

Apples—Keep in dry place as cool as possible without freezing.
Brooms—Hang in the cellar-way to keep soft and pliant.
Cranberries—Keep under water in cellar; change water monthly.
*Dish of hot water set in oven prevents cakes, etc., from scorching.
*Economize time, health, and means, and you will never beg.
Flour—Keep cool, dry, and securely covered.
Glass—Clean with a quart water mixed with tablespoon of ammonia.

Herbs—*Gather when beginning to blossom; keep in paper sacks.*
Ink Stains—*Wet with spirits turpentine; after three hours, rub well.*
Jars—*To prevent, coax "husband" to buy a Buckeye Cook Book.*
Keep an account of all supplies with cost and date when purchased.
Love lightens labor.
Money—*Count carefully when you receive change.*
Nutmegs—*Prick with a pin, and if good, oil will run out.*
Orange and lemon peel—*Dry, pound, and keep in corked bottles.*
Parsnips—*Keep in ground until spring.*
Quicksilver and white of an egg destroy bedbugs.
Rice—*Select large with a clear fresh look; old rice may have insects.*
Sugar—*for general use, the granulated is best.*
Tea—*Equal parts of Japan and green are as good as English breakfast.*
Use a cement made of ashes, salt, and water for cracks in stove.
Variety is the best culinary practice.
Watch your back yard for dirt and bones.
Xantippe was a scold. Don't imitate her.
Youth is best preserved by a cheerful temper.
Zinc-lined sinks are better than wooden ones.

KNOW THE RESULTS OF YOUR SELECTIONS. Furniture, decorations, and other surroundings that are disorderly or in bad taste have a harmful effect on the character of the inmates of a house. The worst effect is upon the impressionable children, who take their own homes as models; what they see in childhood tends to fix their standards for life. Hence, neat, tasteful, and orderly homes have a very important educational influence.

KEEP YOUR HOME IN ORDER. To beautify a home and then freely use it is a duty we owe to that innate love of beauty which God has implanted in us:

- Adorn your house with books, pictures, papers, and enliven it with music.
- Plant trees for shade and trees for fruit; cultivate flowers and shrubbery.
- Keep up the fences.
- Keep the house painted.
- If a gate hinge or a door knob be broken or out of order, repair it at once; let nothing "go to rack."

A steamer of the Morgan line, comfortable and pleasant as ever a steamer can be, carried us to Galveston—a place I had pictured to myself as much larger and grander. But the hotel—though my room did happen to look out on the county jail—was well kept; and some of the streets looked like gardens, from the oleander-trees lining them on either side. The trees were in full blossom, and they gave a very pleasant appearance to the houses, in front of which they stood.

Some few of these houses looked like a piece of fairy-land: nothing could have been built in better taste, nothing could be kept in more perfect order. Too many of them, however, showed the signs of decay and ruin that speak to us with mute pathos of nerveless despair from almost every object in the South.

—"To Texas, And By the Way,"
September 1871

MODEL TASTE AFTER NATURE. Follow nature and good taste will not be offended. Do not encourage shams; let everything be genuine. Do not substitute the grotesque for the graceful or make a sacrifice of comfort to carry out an idea. Do not paint wood to imitate bronze or plaster to look like stone. Remember that there is an eternal fitness in things. Comfort and taste can easily be combined.

The Front Room

Let the front part of the house be thrown open and the most convenient room in it be selected as the family room. Let its doors be ever open; when the work of the kitchen is completed, let mother and daughters be found there with their appropriate work. Even if the family living room be plain, the children leave traces of their growing up in it, and the faces of the old people who have there lived out their lives look down from its walls.

OUTFIT THE ROOM WITH A READING AREA. Let that table, which has always stood under the looking glass, against the wall, be wheeled into the room, its leaves raised, and plenty of useful—not ornamental—books and periodicals be laid upon it. When evening comes bring on the lights, and plenty of them, for sons and daughters, all who can, will be most willing students. They will read; they will learn; they will discuss the subjects of their studies with each other; and parents will often be quite as much instructed as their children.

DECORATE THE GENTLEMAN'S CHAIR. A pretty way to cover the upper part of the back of a handsome chair is with a towel of fine quality and heavily fringed ends. Tie the center of the towel with a ribbon or cord tightly so that the ends of the towel are left hanging like the ends of a necktie; put the tied center of the towel in the middle of the back of the chair and spread the ends out, putting a bow of ribbon at the center where the towel is tied. This is particularly tidy for a gentleman's high-backed chair, as he may lean his head on either side without soiling the chair.

DECORATE THE ROCKING CHAIR. The ugly back of a splint rocking chair can be improved by covering it with a strip of drab linen with a narrow border in outline stitch on each edge. Slip one end between the strips of wood at the top and bring the other end under at the bottom and fasten them securely. They may be kept in place by tying them to the rounds at the top; if done with ribbons this looks pretty.

Austin

April 5, 1891

I'm a little sorry we will have only one "folding door." I'd like one from the parlor into the hall very much; but I can be very contented without it and we don't want to put too much in this house. Aren't you going to have the ground graded? Can't you have it elevated something like the Devees' place? Perhaps it is not worth the expense. That you must decide; but I think it is so lovely and adds tenfold to the place.

—excerpt from a letter from Winifred McCraw
to her betrothed, Patrick Swearingen, in San Antonio

DECORATE THE WALLS EASILY. The cover designs and full-page illustrations of several of the leading monthlies and other periodicals are reproductions of the best works of prominent artists and illustrators. These are freely used in many homes to decorate the walls of libraries, dens, and sometimes living rooms, either framed or bound in passe-partout binding or merely neatly trimmed with a straight-edge and attached to the wall by means of brass-headed tacks or thumb tacks. A series of cover designs of one or more periodicals makes a very interesting and attractive frieze for the den or library.

CONSIDER CALLERS WHEN TIDYING. As a last finishing touch to the rearranging of the parlor, leave late papers, magazines, a volume of poetry, or a stereoscope and views where they will be readily picked up by callers.

The Arm Chair

"**I AM** gouty," said the arm-chair to the mantelpiece and fender,
"You would scarce perhaps believe it, but my left foot is quite tender!

"At our fancy ball last midnight I could hardly step the lancers,
But the ladies were so pressing—they'd not take my 'Nos' for answers!

"There was little round Miss Table, as charming as she's pretty;
And the lovely Lady Fire Screen—to refuse her what a pity!

"Then my dear friend, Sophy Cushion, in her graceful frills and flounces;
Oh what turns we've had together, though the spiteful say she bounces!

"But my dancing days are over, all my days of fun and chatter;
I must be content to sit here and discuss more solid matter."

Here the mantelpiece and fender, by the fireside (as their choice is),
In the praise of quiet converse, to console him raised their voices.

*—Enchanted Tulips and
Other Verses for Children*, 1914

The Dining Room

Of all rooms in the house, the dining room should be the cheeriest, because it is there that all members of the family are most likely to congregate. No matter how widely the interests and occupations of father, mother, and children may separate them at other times of the day, at least one-fifth of their waking hours will probably be spent at the table.

In fitting the dining room, its capacities should be studied. Unless there is ample space, no superfluous ornamentation should be attempted; all desirable room should be given to the necessary furniture. Here is a list of furniture recommended:

TABLE. The table should be firm and solid and not so shaky that the guests fear some catastrophe. Decidedly, square and round tables are the most desirable; because, placed in a circle or nearly facing the host, no guest is given precedence except those who occupy the seats of honor at the right hand of the host and hostess respectively.

CHAIRS. Chairs upholstered with leather are the nicest, and oak chairs with high backs are popular. Chairs can be made absolutely comfortable with practicable cushions; small hassocks can be placed under the table for additional comfort. Cane-seat chairs should never be used in the dining room; they catch beads and fringes and play sad havoc with them. The perforated wood ones are equally bad; the brass-headed nails with which they are fastened catch worse than the cane, and many a delicate fabric has been ruined by them.

SERVING TABLES. A side table for carving will be needed. This carving table can be mounted on rollers so that it can be brought near the dining table when it is required. The sideboard may be of any fancied design which affords the convenience of shelves for plate and table ornaments, and drawers and under-closets for linen, cutlery, plate, and fine glassware. The drawers used for plates and the under-closets should be provided with locks.

CHINA CLOSET. The china cabinet is a useful and beautiful article of furniture, but in the absence of such a cabinet any ordinary closet opening into the dining room may be utilized by replacing its door with a decorative door with diamond panes of glass or with a drapery hanging from a rod and drawn aside when the dining room is in use.

Decor

Once furniture is placed, divert your attention to enhancing the room's atmosphere:

INSTALL AMPLE SOURCES OF WELL-PLACED LIGHT. The ideal dining room is bright with sunlight or lamplight; admit sunshine if possible. In cities, dependence must be placed upon neutral-tinted walls and draperies, enlivened by freshly colored pictures; the light of open fires; and the soft colors of candle flame and shaded lamps.

LOOKING GLASS. When a looking glass or mirror is used, either as part of a sideboard or for wall decoration, care should be taken that no rays of sunlight strike it; their chemical action destroys the perfect distribution of the amalgam with which the reverse of the glass is coated and causes an appearance of granulation or crystallization upon the surface of the mirror.

WALL HANGINGS. Many dining rooms are furnished with dark wood; the walls are gloomy or covered with dismal pictures of dead game and fish. Instead, let the pictures be of fruit or of other still life with bright colors. The most modest establishment admits these possibilities, and from them the plainest repast gains a charm.

The Importance of Thoughtful Appointments

. . . every room was miracle of neatness. Some of them were furnished in the fashion of Mrs. Gray's early days, and the remainder modernized by Clara's taste. She was fond of flowers; her windows were full of pots, and flower-stands were everywhere; she bought books also, novels and poems. Chintz was a weakness with her, and comfortable cushions prevailed, and covered furniture; in short, the whole house had an individual atmosphere pleasing to all.

—"The Tea-Party," October 1871

Rugs. A wooden floor with one or more rugs is preferable to a carpeted floor. Woolen fabrics attract and retain odors; for this reason, as well as upon the score of cleanliness, a movable carpet or rug is better for dining-room use than one nailed to the floor.

Window decorations. When location permits, the windows of the dining room should reflect harmonies of light and color. There can be no more appropriate or enjoyable window decoration than that of stained or painted glass; the infinite variety in form and coloring offered in artistic and lovely designs makes an embarrassment of riches in this form of decoration.

Decorative china. When fine china or old pieces of plate are used in decorating the dining room, they should be disposed above the doors and fireplace on shelves or brackets.

AN UP-TO-DATE

Selected Line in Every Department of Furniture and House Furnishing Goods. Terms: Either cash, or easy weekly or monthly payments. The Ladies especially welcome, whether desiring to purchase or not.

J.M. Mitchell, Proprietor
Austin Funiture Co.,
Phone 80
805 Congress Avenue, Austin, Texas

—Advertisement in *The Capitol Cook Book,* 1899

Sleeping Rooms

PROVIDE SEPARATE BEDS. Where two persons sleep in the same bed, the one who has the stronger physical power is likely to absorb the vital forces of the weaker one. Where either is afflicted with any tendency toward consumption, has any skin disease, or other malady, he is likely to impart its evil influences, if not its actual contagion, to the person who shares his bed with him.

OUTFIT BEDROOMS WITH:

Bed slips. Bed linen often falls short of covering the mattress completely while in use; hence, the extra slip is needed, especially to protect from dust the underside of the mattress. These slips can be removed and laundered, twice a year or oftener, when housecleaning; pillow covers may be removed oftener if desired. Ticking treated in this way will be fresh and clean at the end of a dozen years' hard usage, when otherwise it would be so worn and soiled as to be unfit for use.

Linen sheets. Linen is, of course, the best material for comfort, appearance, and durability; but cotton sheeting is more commonly used because it is less expensive. Buy unbleached linen or cotton for sheets and pillow covers, as it is not only less expensive, but much more durable and can be easily bleached when being laundered.

Feathers. The best feathers for beds and pillows are feathers plucked from live birds. Chicken, goose, or duck feathers may be preserved and used for beds or pillows by putting all the soft feathers together in a barrel as they are picked from the birds after scalding. Leave the barrel open to the sun and rain, covering it with an old screen to prevent the feathers from blowing about.

Pillow-sham holder and lifter. Few articles of household use have been introduced that are as indispensable to ladies who pride themselves on having neat, tidy houses as the sham holder, a neat solution to the question of what to do with the shams at night. The holder consists of a light frame readily attached to any bedstead, upon which the shams are pinned or sewed to a tape and are held in their proper position during the day, either with or without a pillow under them. At night, by means of a spring, they are instantly raised up against the headboard of the bed, entirely out of the way of the sleeper.

SLEEP OUT OF DOORS IF POSSIBLE. Probably no practice would be more invigorating, healthful, or pleasurable than sleeping out of doors. In the vicinity of the great sanitariums, where sleeping out of doors has been proved to be a cure for consumption and other diseases, many persons have formed the habit of sleeping thus. Any porch somewhat excluded from view and in a sheltered location can be utilized. The porch should be screened and provided with storm curtains of tent canvas that can be drawn and buttoned like the curtains of a carriage.

Living out of doors

Miscellaneous Receipts for the Household

Remedies for Household Pests

- Cayenne pepper will keep the storeroom and pantry free from *ants* and *cockroaches*.
- For *bugs* and *ants,* one may also dissolve 2 pounds alum in 3 quarts boiling water. Apply boiling hot with a brush. Add alum to whitewash for storerooms, pantries, and closets.
- Kerosene oil is a sure remedy for *red ants*. Place small blocks under a sugar barrel, so as not to let the oil touch the barrel.

- Uncork a bottle of oil of pennyroyal, and it will drive away *mosquitoes* or other blood-sucking insects; they will not return so long as the scent of it is in the room.
- Mix a little powdered potash with meal and throw it into the rat holes and it will not fail to drive the *rats* away.
- If a *mouse* enters into any part of your dwelling, saturate a rag with cayenne in solution and stuff it into his hole.

To Remove Bugs

TO REMOVE BEDBUGS

The most certain way to destroy bedbugs is to put the bedstead into a closed room and set fire to the following composition, placed in an iron pot upon the hearth, having previously closed up the chimney, then shut the door; let them remain a day.

Sulphur, 10 parts; saltpeter, powdered, 1 part. Mix.

Be sure to open the door of the room five or six hours before you venture to go into it a second time.

TO REMOVE CRICKETS

Put a little chloride of lime and powdered tobacco in their holes.

—*Wright's Book of 3000 Practical Receipts*, 1869

Cleaning and Polishing Furniture and Utensils

TO CLEAN COPPER WARE. Wash and rub with half a lemon. Take a handful of common salt and enough vinegar and flour to make a paste, then mix together thoroughly. There is nothing better for cleaning coppers. After using the paste, wash thoroughly with hot water, rinse in cold water, and wipe dry.

TO CLEAN ENAMELED WARE. Dampen a cloth, dip it in common soda, rub the ware briskly, wash and wipe dry. Or keep them clean by rubbing with sifted wood ashes or whitening. Care must be taken not to use lye in cleaning tins, as it will injure them

TO CLEAN EARTHENWARE. Put in a kettle with cold water, ashes, and sal soda, bring to a boil, and after boiling let stand 24 hours in the lye; or fill the vessels with hot lime water and let them stand 24 hours.

TO PREVENT LIME DEPOSITS. A clean oyster shell put in the tea kettle will attract sediments that are deposited from boiling water and will thus prevent an unpleasant crust from gathering on the inside of the tea kettle.

Not long ago I listened to a very charming talk ... entitled "The Home Gymnasium" ... She said one could scrub the table and obtain the best exercise for arms and chest, and at the same time produce an article or piece of furniture which would be a delight to the eye in its whiteness and brightness. She said that in scrubbing the floor one obtained very much the same movement that would be given in the gymnasium, while at the same time the exercise would conduce not only to the personal advantage but to the happiness of the family.

—*What a Young Woman Ought to Know,* 1898

TO CLEAN GLASSWARE. Fill with buttermilk, let stand 48 hours, and wash in soapsuds. Or, put in 2 tablespoons of vinegar and 1 tablespoon of baking soda. This will effervesce vigorously. Hold the article over the sink; if a decanter, do not cork or the vessel may burst.

TO REMOVE THE YELLOW DISCOLORATION OF CHINA. Moisten a soft cloth in water and dip into dry salt, fine coal, or wood ashes and rub off the stain with it. Afterwards, wash with soap and water.

To clean draperies. Draperies and tapestries hung upon the walls may be cleaned by pouring gasoline into a shallow pan and brushing them with this by means of a soft brush or whisk broom.

To polish hardwood floors. Chip up finely not quite a ½ pound of beeswax and put it on the stove to melt. When melted, pour it in one quart of turpentine and add five cents' worth ammonia. Then set it in a tin pail of hot water and stir the polish over the fire until thoroughly blended. Remember that all these ingredients are highly flammable, and guard against their taking fire. See that the hardwood floor is perfectly clean, dry, and free from dust; then apply the polish to it with a soft woolen cloth, rubbing it well into the grain of the wood. After the polish is applied to the floor, rub it very hard with a polishing brush. Polish two or three times a week.

To clean furniture. Mix a ½ pint of linseed oil, a ½ pint of vinegar, and a ½ pint of turpentine. Apply with a flannel rag and then rub with a dry flannel.

To polish furniture. Mix 1 pint of alcohol, 1 pint of spirits of turpentine, 1½ pints of raw linseed oil, 1 ounce balsam fir, and 1 ounce ether. Cut the balsam with the alcohol, which will take about 12 hours. (That is to say, dilute the balsam with the alcohol.) Mix the oil with the turpentine in a separate vessel and add the alcohol, and last the ether. Apply with a woolen cloth.

Chapter Nine

For the Cook Appointing Her Kitchen

There are very few housekeepers indeed who could not—by intelligent forethought in planning and arranging the contents of the kitchen, pantry, and storeroom—save themselves daily miles of useless traveling to and fro.

Furniture

Begin with the correct furniture:

Stove. First, the housekeeper must have a good stove or range, and it is well for her to have the dealer at hand when it is put up, to see that it draws well. A piece of hard, smooth asbestos board under the range, cook stove, parlor stove, gas stove, or small oil stove is superior to iron or zinc because it is durable, easier to keep clean, and presents a better appearance. The woodwork near stoves and the collars above stovepipes, where they pass through the ceiling and walls, may be protected by the same material.

Ovens. Separate ovens should be used for meat and pastry because the particles of fat which fly from the meat while it is baking burn upon the sides of the oven and impart their odor and flavor to delicate cakes and pastry. The bread and pastry ovens do not require to be so hot as those in which meat is baked, and means must be devised to moderate their heat when it is excessive. All the flues and the top and bottom of the ovens should be kept free from ashes, and the dampers should always be in good working order.

SINK. The sink may be of iron or other metal, stone, or even wood lined with lead, tin, or zinc. But it should stand on four legs. The sink should be placed high enough so that the dishes may be washed without stooping. A small shelf or cupboard above the sink to contain soap, borax, washing powder, and various utensils will be found convenient.

SINK-SIDE WORK TABLE. A bench or table, homemade if necessary, at the left of the kitchen sink and as large as the room will admit, is indispensable. Have the table overlap the edge of the sink and cover it with zinc, which will not rust. Turn up the zinc over a molding around the sides of the table, except at the end over the sink, so that water will drain back from it into the latter. Carry the zinc, if possible, 18 inches or 2 feet up the kitchen wall behind the table and the sink. This is lasting, easily kept clean, and is not injured by hot pans or kettles. If scrubbed clean it can be used as a molding board; particles of dough which adhere to it can easily be scraped off with a knife.

Air is admitted to every part

A Southern kitchen and pantry are a study for a Northerner. In the first place you notice two or three cupboards with doors of wire net. These doors are to keep out the flying cockroaches and the clouds of innumerable gnats and flies of 20 different species, which are blown heedlessly about by every breeze into all corners, or which deliberately follow their noses—if they have noses—in quest of bread, meat, pastry, sugar, or anything good to eat or to drink. And if you look lower you will see that every cupboard and every table there and in the dining room has a shallow tin dish set under each of its feet, and that each dish is full of water. That is to keep the ants which swarm over the floor from mounting higher.

—"Among the Insects in a Southern City," July 1885

TABLEWARE CABINET. Placing a china cabinet for the ordinary tableware just above the sink-side work table saves time and steps lost in walking from the sink to the table, and thence to pantry or closet.

STOOL. Provide a strong stool, high enough to allow sitting down at the sink to pare vegetables and for other purposes.

WORK TABLE. The kitchen table may be used as a work table if covered with oilcloth. This will last a long time if the table is padded with sheet wadding or several thicknesses of newspaper covered with an old sheet. Draw the padding smooth and tack it under the edge of the table.

KITCHEN CABINET. A good kitchen cabinet with metal bins for flour, meal, and other substances that mice are fond of is an investment which will save time and strength for the housekeeper and will be a money-saver in the long run. These bins should be removable so that they can be regularly washed, scalded, and dried.

Footstool. A footstool, convenient also as a receptacle for work, may be made of a common pine soap box; fasten the cover on the box with small hinges and put on the bottom four small castors. Line the box with plain white paper and cover. Excelsior, which can be got at any furniture store, is good to stuff the top and much cheaper than curled hair.

Other Useful Objects to Have About

For your own or your cook's convenience, provide your kitchen with:

Washboard. Hang beside the sink a small washboard to rub out dishcloths and keep towels sweet and clean.

Dish drain. Make a dish drain from an old dishpan by perforating the bottom with holes by means of a hammer and round wire nails. Place the draining pan to the left of the dishpan to avoid unnecessary handling. If the handles are front and back, as you face the dishpan, you will have fewer pieces of nicked china. If lye is used, and the dishwater is fairly hot and soapy, dishes rinsed with cold water will dry in the rack bright and shiny and not require wiping. Or, if thoroughly rinsed with hot water, they may be allowed to drain the same way.

Slate. A child's school slate hung on a nail, with a slate pencil attached by a strong cord, will be found a great convenience in ordering groceries. When any supplies run low, make a note on the slate of what is wanted; when the grocer calls, run over this list to refresh your mind. The slate is also useful for making a program each morning of the things to be done through the day. You will be surprised to find how quickly these things will be disposed of. When cooking or preparing company dinner, make a list of the articles to be prepared.

Toppers. Keep a nice flat-washed rock to weight down butter, beef, or tongues under brine; and stiff writing paper to dip in brandy and lay on top of preserves.

Dinner mats. Dinner mats, either square or oval, made of two thicknesses of linen with an opening at one end to admit a square of asbestos, will prevent the hot tea or coffee pot or dishes containing hot food from injuring the tablecloth or the polished surface of the table.

Stove mats. Asbestos mats lined with wire have many uses about the stove. They may be placed in a hot oven to prevent cakes and pies from burning on the bottom and also on the top of the stove to prevent the contents of kettles and saucepans from burning. A small wire-lined asbestos mat, with a hole cut through the center but not through the wire, will be found useful for warming milk and other things in cups and small saucepans with rounded bottoms. The heat is applied to the bottom instead of the sides, and the vessel will not tip.

Stove holders. At least a half dozen stove holders are not too many to have at hand in the kitchen at all times. Sew brass curtain rings and hang on a nail near the stove holders made of strong washable material, such as ticking or worn-out overalls, containing a removable square of asbestos. Or a large pair of loose mittens of canvas lined with asbestos may be fastened to a cord about two feet long and, when much cooking is to be done, slipped under the apron band so that both are suspended and always at hand.

Match safe. Keep a stock of matches on a high, dry shelf in a covered earthen jar or tin box with a tight lid where they will be out of the way of children and safe from rats and mice. These animals are fond of phosphorus and will gnaw match heads if they can and often set them on fire. Have a covered match safe in each room where they are in frequent use; match safes fastened to sandpaper will be found a great convenience.

Ash receptacle. Keep a sheet-iron pan or scuttle to take up ashes.

Sleeve protectors. An old pair of stockings may be converted into useful sleeve protectors by cutting off the feet and hemming the cut edge. These may be drawn over the sleeves of a clean gown if necessary when washing dishes.

DISHCLOTHS. Save and use cloth flour, sugar, salt, and cornmeal sacks, which keep white and last longer than ordinary towel stuff. You may also use scrim or cotton underwear crocheted about the edge or folded and hemmed double or the fiber of the so-called dishrag gourd, the seeds of which may be obtained from any seedman. Cheesecloth is good both for washing and wiping dishes, especially for drying silver and glassware.

STOCK THE KITCHEN WITH SUCH CONTAINERS AS:

- Milk vessels of tin or earthenware, never stoneware
- Four buckets with close-fitting lids for setting aside milk for later—one for dinner, one for supper, one for breakfast, one for cooking purposes
- Bottles and jugs to hold yeast while rising and walnut catsup while sunning
- Stone jars to fill with brine in which to throw lemon peels to suit one's convenience and to store pickles, pack with shad, spices, and vinegar to set in boiling water for potted shad
- Demijohn or runlet for storing wine
- Glass jars for keeping preserves so they can be readily inspected
- Firkin to hold rolls of butter and to keep boiled pigs feet closely covered to prevent them from molding before they are fried
- Preserving kettle to put up corn in brine
- Small, common glasses for keeping jellies
- Wide-mouthed glass jars for keeping marmalade
- Piggin for taking up butter
- Cotton bags to hang plum pudding for keeping

The Storeroom

Groceries and supplies for a household of any size should, if possible, be bought in quantity; therefore, every house should have a storeroom, appointed as follows.

MAKE A STOREROOM INEXPENSIVELY. A small storeroom can be made in a corner of the cellar at much less cost than is commonly supposed by putting up walls of concrete made of sand or gravel and cement. When furnished with a suitable door, this storeroom will be damp-proof and free from dust, germs, and all other unsanitary pests. There should be a cellar window protected on the outside by wire netting and having on the inside a removable screen of cheesecloth to keep out the dust. If you would have wholesome food, keep the window down at the top, night and day, except in the coldest weather.

INCLUDE AMPLE SHELVING. Slat shelves painted with white paint and a coat of enamel may be built up in the storeroom back to back, with just enough room between them for a person to walk, in the same manner as book stacks in a library. Preserves, pickles, canned goods, butter, eggs, and other groceries can be stored year-round in perfect safety.

HANG NETS FOR FRUIT. A suspended net or two should also be supplied for hanging lemons and oranges.

STOCK THE ROOM WITH EARTHENWARE. Earthenware jars are necessary for sugar, oatmeal, rice, tapioca, sago, barley, and spices. And, if it is wished to keep on hand the pound cake and fruit cake of our grandmothers (some cakes made from old-fashioned recipes given in this book will keep for years), no snugger quarters for their preservation can be found than earthen jars with tight-fitting lids inside the dry storeroom.

Keep an account book. This is the room where you should enter the date when each item is bought and the price paid for it in your account book.

Make an outdoor cupboard. Have you an outdoor cupboard in which to keep milk, meat, and fish during the cool weather of early spring and fall? A dry-goods box with a hinged locked door, nailed above the reach of cats and dogs against the arbor that covers the kitchen door, will save many a journey to the storeroom. It should have holes bored in the ends to allow a current to circulate through it, for food will keep fresher and sweeter in the open air.

Chapter Ten

For the Homemaker on the Grounds

In the Garden

I wish all my fair sisters would set apart a portion of their home grounds for the garden.

CONSIDER THE ECONOMIC BENEFITS. An area of land cultivated as a kitchen garden will easily supply the family table with $100 worth of vegetables every year.

CULTIVATE A FLOWER GARDEN FOR WELL-BEING. Best for the lady who tends the garden is that life-giving something in the very smell of the ground, especially in the soft springtime. And when long summer days come, when the lady drops her endless sewing and gathers what she has grown in anticipation of preparing a fresh meal, a vase of colorful blooms upon the table to meet the family when they sit will give her a lighter step and rosy cheeks. This is not romance but sound common sense.

START SMALL. Most women have their time quite fully occupied with the supervision of household matters. They would like to have some flowers, because a certain amount of work among them is refreshing, a resting spell because of its change from the monotony of work indoors. The cultivation of a small garden will not involve more labor than they can perform in odd spells, but if they attempt too much, the flowers will call for so much attention that the idea of rest and recreation is destroyed and they will fail to enjoy them. Begin cautiously and enlarge the operation as you feel justified in doing so.

PREPARE SOIL CAREFULLY. To prepare earth for seeds or small plants or for filling pots or window boxes, mix one part by bulk of well-rotted manure, two parts of good garden loam, and one part of sharp fine sand. Choose for this purpose manure which has been thoroughly rotted but not exposed to leaching from the weather. Mix all together in a heap, stir well with the shovel, sift and place in bores or in the bed prepared for the seed. If convenient, bake the soil for an hour in a hot oven. This will kill all weed seed and spores of fungous disease.

PROTECT PLANTS FROM THE WEATHER. To protect small plants from heat drive stakes into the ground slanting toward the north and lean boards against them to shade the rows. Or use light frames on lath or wooden slate and cover them with cotton cloth. To protect crops planted in winter from cold and give an early start in spring, set the stakes slanting to the south and lean boards against them on the north side. Or cover with a mulch of manure, straw, or leaves. But take care that this is not so thick as to keep the air from the plants.

To a passerby the domain presented a cheerful view; order was established everywhere.... Clara's pansies and tulips trembled in the flowing airs. Hens clucked in the garden, and scrambled after a man who was turning up the clods. The necessary cat, instigated by the song of a robin, scampered up and down the palings, watched by a big dog, who lay on the terrace, his paws crossed in lazy content.

—"The Tea-Party," 1871

Adornment

Among the many objects used for adornment, there is a very pretty one which we would like to see more frequently employed, and which when properly placed by the side of some walk well retired from other objects, is in itself highly suggestive. We refer to the sundial. What thoughts this monitor suggests to the mind! How silent, yet how eloquent! His must be a vacant mind indeed who can pass such a teacher without finding thought to accompany his walk. A shadow teacheth us, and we learn in the end that we have pursued but shadows.

—*Woodward's Architecture and Rural Art*, 1867

CHOOSE OLD SEED DEALERS. If you send to the florist for seed—and it is always advisable to do that, for he makes a specialty of seed growing and knows how to produce the best—be sure to patronize a reliable dealer. There are always men in all kinds of business who are not to be trusted. The old seed farms are all reliable, I think; their continuance in business proves that, for if they were not they would, after a little, lose customers and give up.

FORM A SEED CLUB. The packages of seeds put up by most seed growers generally contain more than one person will use. It is a good plan to club together in a country neighborhood. The cost will be less, and there will be seeds enough to divide among half a dozen persons.

PLANT RASPBERRIES, BLACKBERRIES, CURRANTS, GOOSEBERRIES, AND GRAPES IN THE FALL. These fruits set out in fall, even in October, before the leaf drops, will make double the growth and double the fruit the next year than if planted in spring. I recommend early setting so that fall rains may settle the dirt nicely about the roots, and the fruits begin their growth with the opening of spring, even throwing out rootlets in the fall. Mulch before freezing with litter of any kind—manure, sawdust, sods, or straw—over each hill and they will come out all right in spring and begin to grow as soon as frost is out, scarcely a plant failing.

In the Barn and On the Farm

As the care and maintenance of domestic animals most frequently falls to the supervision of the farmwife, keep these brief thoughts in mind.

TREAT YOUR ANIMALS WITH KINDNESS. Curse and scream at them and you excite their fears and injure their disposition to be kind. A pet today and a kick tomorrow will destroy their confidence in you and leads them to expect abuse rather than kindness.

Letter from the Wife of a Settler Who Cannot Settle

Dear Elizabeth,

*My dear Simson has concluded to settle in America, and we are now on our way thither, on board of the Great Western. . . . Simson, dear fellow, is full of plans and rural felicity, and we clear a farm, erect our buildings, and grow rich every day, sometimes in one place and sometimes in another, but have not yet made up our minds where.
. . . Texas, they say, is a perfect paradise, and land is so uncommonly cheap that you can buy a farm for the price of a new bonnet, but earthquakes are very common, and the people so very cruel. They kill each other with bowie knives in the streets in open day, and so reckless that they keep singing "Welcome to your gory bed," as if it was fine sport, so we have had to abandon all idea of it, as it would be mere madness to go there.*

—*The Letter-Bag of the Great Western,* 1873

BEWARE THE IMPATIENCE OF BOYS AND HIRED HELP. They are likely to think there is no way of showing their power over a horse but by jerking at the reins and yelling or cursing at him.

DON'T KEEP THOSE YOU CAN'T FEED. One well-wintered horse is worth as much as two that drag through on straw. The same is true of oxen, and emphatically so of cows. The owner of a half-starved dog loses the use of him, for at the very time when he is most needed as a guard, he must be off scouring the country for food.

KEEP YOUR ANIMALS CLEAN. Cleanliness is indispensable, if one would keep his animals healthy. In their state all our domestic animals are very clean and very healthy. The hog is not naturally a dirty animal, but quite the reverse. He enjoys currying as much as a horse or cow, and would be as careful of his litter as a cat if he had a fair chance.

Austin

April 3, 1891

I'm delighted that you bought a horse and one so well-suited to all. How many, many pleasant, joyful hours I anticipate with you, especially driving with you behind our own horse!

—Excerpt from a letter from Winifred McCraw
to her betrothed, Patrick Swearingen,
in San Antonio

REMEMBER, WHEN MILKING:
- Put the fingers around the teat close to the bag.
- Firmly close the forefingers of each hand alternately, immediately squeezing with the other fingers (the forefingers prevent the milk flowing back into the bag, while the others press it out).
- Sit with the left knee close to the right hind leg of the cow and the head pressed against her flank.

- Keep the left hand always ready to ward off a blow from her feet, which the gentlest cow may give almost without knowing it, if her tender teats be cut by long nails or her bag be tender.
- Strip her dry every time she is milked, or she will dry up.
- If she gives much milk, it pays to milk three times a day.

Hints on Poultry Raising

- Do not feed fowls too much soft, wet feed; it is liable to affect their digestive organs. Grit, shell, dry bone, and charcoal, while perhaps not proper foods, are important accessories in raising fowls.
- Oyster shells should be given to pullets when they show signs of laying, and should be always accessible to laying hens.
- If you have not already received it, send for "Dr. Sloan's Advice" on the care and treatment of Horses, Cattle, Hogs, and Poultry. It tells how to cure Bramble-foot, Cholera, Diarrhea, Roup, and Worms with Sloan's Liniment and how to rid hens of lice.

—*Sloan's Cook Book and Advice to Housekeepers*, 1905

The most absorbing part of the "Woman's question" of the present time is the remedy for the varied sufferings of women who are widows or unmarried, and without means of support.... A woman can invest capital in the dairy and qualify herself to superintend a dairy farm as well as a man.... And, too, the raising of poultry, of hogs, and of sheep are all within the reach of a woman with proper abilities and training for this business. So that, if a woman chooses, she can find employment both interesting and profitable in studying the care of domestic animals.

—*Miss Beecher's Housekeeper and Healthkeeper*, 1873

Miscellaneous Receipts for the Barn and Farm

TO FATTEN PIGS VERY FAT. Feed them on boiled rice.

TO GATHER AND PRESERVE ROOTS. Roots should be gathered in spring, with but few exceptions, and are better for being fresh. Roots to be dried should be well washed and sliced, unless they are preserved for the sake of the bark, when they must be merely washed and dried. The process of drying may be simply performed by stringing the pieces together, or scattering them on paper trays, and exposing them, for a sufficient time, to a gentle heat, say from 90 to 130 degrees Fahrenheit.

TO PROCURE ICE. Nearly fill a gallon stone bottle with hot spring water (leaving room for about a pint), and put in two ounces of refined nitre; the bottle must then be stopped very close and let down into a deep well. After three or four hours it will be completely frozen, but the bottle must be broken to procure the ice. If the bottle is moved up and down, so as to be sometimes in and sometimes out of the water, the consequent evaporation will hasten the process.

COMPOSITION TO HEAL WOUNDS IN TREES. Mix four parts chalk, two parts tar, and one part brick dust. Melt and apply warm.

TO DRIVE BUGS FROM VINES. The ravage of the yellow-striped bug on cucumbers and melons may be prevented by sifting charcoal dust over the plants; if repeated three or four times, the plants will be entirely freed from annoyance. There is in charcoal some property so noxious to these troublesome insects, that they fly from it the instant it is applied.

TO NOURISH A FARM HORSE AT WORK. A small horse that is driven or worked should have 2 quarts at a feed, given 3 times a day, with 5 pounds of hay (cut), night and morning. And a horse that is not working, but will be soon, would be the better for a daily feed of 2 quarts of grain (oats) given at noon. An excellent mixture of grain is cracked 1 bushel corn and 2 bushels oats.

TO SAVE OATS IN FEEDING HORSES. Bruise or crush your oats in a mill, and your horse will become fatter on half his usual allowance of these oats than he was before on double the quantity unprepared. If you cannot bruise the oats, pour hot water on them and let them soak for a few hours.

TO CURE THE RED WATER IN CATTLE. Take 1 ounce Armenian bole, a ½ ounce dragon's blood, 2 ounces Castile soap, and 1 dram rock-alum. Dissolve these in a quart of hot ale or beer, and let it stand until it is blood-warm. Give this as one dose, and, if it should have the desired effect, give the same quantity about 12 hours after. This is an excellent medicine for changing the water and acts as a purgative.

WARTS ON COWS' TEATS OR THE HAND'S REMEDY. Take a handful of green bean leaves and rub them in the hands until the hands are thoroughly wet with the juice; then proceed to milk. As often as the hands get dry while milking, moisten again with the bean leaf juice. Do this twice or three times a week, and in a few weeks there will be no warts on the cow's teats or the hands of the milker.

SIMPLE BUT CERTAIN REMEDY FOR EGG-EATING HENS. Make an opening in the large end of an egg and let out the contents, beat them up, mix into them enough strong mustard to refill the egg, and paste on a bit of cloth to keep the contents in. Then place the egg where the egg-eaters can see and get at it. They will "go for it" at once and as quickly go away. It is too much for them. And as they take it for granted that all eggs are alike, they give up the habit. I cannot see why it would not be as good for egg-eating dogs as for hens.

Chapter Eleven

For the Cook at Her Tasks

Preparing Common Foods

Herein, rather than giving recipes for specific dishes—those come later in the book—I have imparted bits of wisdom earned with experience regarding general preparation of the foods we most often consume. These are matters often taken for granted by cooks of some years and left out of so many recipes. These thoughts follow no particular system; they are simply notable observations made during my life.

Bread

"When the bread rises in the oven, the heart of the housewife rises with it." The speaker of this truth might have added that the heart of the housewife sinks in sympathy with the sinking bread. Bread is so vitally important an element in our nourishment that I have assigned to it the first place in my work.

BE NOT DAUNTED. I would recommend that the housekeeper acquire the practice as well as the theory of bread making. If circumstances should throw her out of a cook for a short time, she is then prepared for the emergency. In this country, fortunes are so rapidly made and lost, the vicissitudes of life are so sudden, that we know not what a day may bring forth. On the other hand, there is no reason why the food of the poor should not be as well prepared and palatable as that of the wealthy. For, by care and pains, the finest bread may be made of the simplest materials, and surely the loving hands of the poor man's wife and daughter will take as much pains to make his bread nice and light as hirelings will do for the wealthy.

To Make Home Happy

The most important of all things pertaining to the Kitchen and Cookery, to happiness and Health, is the "Staff of Life," otherwise GOOD BREAD and BISCUITS, to say nothing of the thousand and one delicacies of Cakes, Waffles, Puddings, Pies, etc., that the children love so much, and which, when well made and properly cooked, are no detriment to health, but are, on the contrary, both nourishing and of the greatest value in giving variety to the somewhat monotonous routine of Meat and Vegetables that go to make up the Bill of Fare of the average American family.

—*Cow Brand Soda Cook Book and Facts Worth Knowing*, 1900

USE GOOD FLOUR. Good flour is an indispensable requisite to good bread and, next, good yeast and sufficient kneading. Only experience will enable you to be a good judge of flour. One test is to rub the dry flour between your fingers; if the grains feel round, it is a sign that the flour is good. If after trying a barrel of flour twice, you find it becomes wet and sticky, after being made up of the proper consistency, you had better then return it to your grocer.

SUN AND AIR FLOUR BEFORE USE. In the morning, get out the flour to be made up at night for next morning's breakfast. Sift it in a tray and put it out in the sun, or, if the day is damp, set it near the kitchen fire.

To Make Good Yeast

Take 5 or 6 good-sized potatoes, then pour 2 quarts of boiling water to them, also drop in a small handful of hops tied in a bag. Take potatoes out when done and mash them, take out hops, then make 1½ teacups of flour in a smooth paste and stir in the hop tea; let boil 5 minutes. Then put in the mashed potatoes, take off the fire, and put in a ½ cup of good yeast or leaven. Keep in a warm place till it rises well, then tie up close and put away till needed, or make leaven.

—*The Capitol Cook Book, 1899*

SET BREAD TO RISE BY SEASON. Set bread to rise in a cool place in summer but in a warm place, free from draughts, in winter. In the latter season, the crock may be wrapped in a blanket or set on bread-warming shelf under which a lighted coal-oil lamp is placed.

HANDLE DOUGH LIGHTLY. Never knead bread a second time after it rises, as this ruins it. Handle as lightly as possible, make into the desired shapes, and put into the molds in which it is to be baked. Use a little lard on the hands when making out the loaf, or else dip a feather in lard and pass lightly over the bread just before putting it in the oven to bake, so as to keep the crust from being too hard. The top must be pricked or cut across so that the crust will not bind. Let it be a little warmer during the second rise than during the first. Always shape and put in the molds two hours before breakfast.

LEARN OVEN PLACEMENT. Set bread on the floor of the stove, never on the shelf since the air is hot at the top of the oven. If you bake your dough hard on top first it would not rise at all, and we wish to have the yeast swell the starch and send the water that is in the dough in steam out through the holes we pricked in the loaf. As you set the bread in the stove, lay a piece of stiff writing paper over it to keep it from browning before heating through. Leave the door ajar a few minutes, then remove the paper and shut the door.

CHECK FOR DONENESS. When the top of the loaf is a light amber color, put back the paper so the bread may not brown too much while thoroughly baking. Turn the mold around so that each part may be exposed to equal heat. Have an empty baking pan on the shelf above the bread to prevent it from blistering. When a broom straw will pass through and come out dry, it is done.

INTRODUCE VARIETY. Do not constantly make bread in the same shapes; each morning, try to have some variation. Plain light bread dough may be made into loaves, rolls, twists, turnovers, and light biscuits; these changes of shape make a pleasant and appetizing variety in the appearance of the table. Very pretty iron shapes (eight or twelve in a group, joined together) may be procured from almost any tinner.

> *More* common sense is required in bread making than in any other branch of cooking. On account of different grades of soda, cream of tartar, baking powder, and yeast, it is impossible to be accurate as to the exact amount to use.
>
> Where sour milk is used, a young cook had just as well make up her mind to taste uncooked bread, so as to ascertain whether there is not enough or too much soda, as this is the only way to succeed every time.
>
> —*The Capitol Cook Book,* 1899

Tea and Coffee

BOIL DIFFERENT TEA TYPES FOR DIFFERENT TIMES. Of all "cups that cheer," there is nothing like the smoking hot cup of tea, made with boiling water, in a thoroughly scalded teapot. And if it is the good old-fashioned green tea of "ye ancient time," you must just put it to draw and not to boil; if it is genuine "English Breakfast" or best black tea, the water must not only be boiling hot, at the very moment of pouring it on, but the tea must actually boil for at least five or ten minutes.

You drank your turbid coffee with no milk to soften its dregginess, and a damp article of brown sugar only to sweeten it. I never could look upon so much squalor and short-commons where wealth—really immense wealth—was, without wondering that the wealthy owner did not force a sale, even in the dullest times, and realize at least enough to repair his roof and provide a proper coffee-pot; or, in flush times, go to the length of a purchase of a dairy-maid. With 20,000 cows, neither milk nor butter could have been an extravagance . . . Still, this would have been an innovation in Texas ideas, and possibly have subjected a man to suspicion as to his loyalty.

—"Leaving Texas," 1874

MAKE A TEAPOT BONNET. To insure "keeping hot" while serving, make the simple contrivance known as a "bonnet" which is warranted a "sure preventive" against that most insipid of all drinks—"a warmish cup of tea." It is merely a sack with a loose elastic in the bottom large enough to cover and encircle the entire teapot. Make it with odd pieces of silk, satin, or cashmere, lined, quilted, and embroidered, if you like; draw this over the teapot as soon as the tea is poured into it.

Milk and Butter

The most exquisite nicety and care must be observed in the management of milk and butter.

KEEP ON HAND TWO SETS OF VESSELS. A housekeeper should have two sets of milk vessels (tin or earthenware, never stoneware, as this is an absorbent). She should never use twice in succession the same milk vessels without having them scalded and aired.

SET ASIDE PLENTY. In warm weather, sweet milk should be set on ice or in a spring house. Never put ice in sweet milk; this dilutes it. One pan of milk should always be set aside to raise cream for coffee. One bucket with a close-fitting lid should be filled with milk and set aside for dinner, one for supper, one for breakfast, and a fourth for cooking purposes.

CHURN CAREFULLY. To make butter, strain unskimmed milk into a scalded churn, where the churning is done daily. This will give a sweeter butter and nicer buttermilk than when cream is skimmed and kept for churning. Do not let the milk in the churn exceed blood heat. If overheated, butter will be white and frothy and milk thin and sour. Churn as soon as the milk is turned. In summer, churn early in the morning, as fewer flies are swarming then, and the butter can be made much firmer.

The coast counties of Texas hardly fulfill the rather boastful claim of the State to the title of the Italy of America. . . . Oranges, grapes, and even peaches, rumored to have existed at some prior date, are now extinct . . . the only fruit at all common, the familiar dried apple; the only milk, the condensed article in cans; the only butter, an importation from the North. . . . This in a country pre-eminently a grazing region, where the cows would cover a thousand hills—if there were any hills to cover.

. . . But do not let it be supposed that such luxuries as dried apples, condensed milk, and stalwart butter are to be found generally. They are strictly confined to the few cities and large towns. I have broken bread—shattered corn-dodger would be more accurate—under the leaky roof of the owner of 40,000 head of cattle, where the use of milk and butter was apparently unknown.

. . . Perhaps I am making life in Texas look rather shady, but it was shady as I saw it, in antebellum days and under the impending shadow of the war—a shadow which withered up the railroad-building enterprise I had come to further. . .

—"Leaving Texas," 1874

SCALD THE CHURN. A stone churn is in some respects more convenient than a wooden churn; but no matter which you use, the most fastidious

> ☞
>
> *Yet* the process of making good butter is a very simple one. To keep the cream in a perfectly pure, cool atmosphere, to churn while it is yet sweet, to work out the buttermilk thoroughly, and to add salt with such discretion as not to ruin the fine, delicate flavor of the fresh cream—all this is quite simple, so simple that one wonders at thousands and millions of pounds of butter yearly manufactured which are merely a hobgoblin-bewitchment of cream into foul and loathsome poisons.
>
> —Harriett Beecher Stowe, *House and Home Papers*, 1869

neatness must be observed. Have the churn scalded and set out to sun as soon as possible after churning. Use your last-made butter for buttering bread, reserving the staler for cookery.

PRINT AND REFRIGERATE CORRECTLY. Butter should be printed early in the morning, while it is cool. A plateful for each of the three meals should be placed in the refrigerator. Do not set butter in a refrigerator or a safe with anything else in it but milk. It readily imbibes the flavor of everything near it.

Eggs

While eggs are nourishing, they are not so heating to the blood as meat, and doctors often order them for patients who need nourishment yet cannot have their blood heated by meat juices. Even when they cost the most, you can really get more nourishment from them than for the same amount of money spent for meat.

TRY SHIRRING EGGS. This is a modification of baking eggs. Butter small earthen dishes and put an egg into each one without mixing the white and yolk; dust a little salt and pepper over the eggs. The eggs should be covered with buttered paper to prevent browning on the surface. The dishes are then placed upon the back of the stove or in a moderate oven. When the whites of the eggs are set, the dishes are then sent to the table and the eggs eaten from them.

TRY VARIOUS OMELETS. There is an infinite variety of omelets, named from the special flavor or seasoning given by any predominating ingredient. The sweet light omelets are used either for breakfast or plain desserts; the plain omelets are suitable for breakfast and luncheon. In parsley and fine herb omelets, the chopped herbs are mixed with the eggs before the omelet is cooked; grated ham, tongue, and cheese are also mixed in the same way. In many other omelets, the special ingredient used is enclosed in the omelet.

DYE EGGS FOR EASTER. Easter morning would be incomplete, for the children at least, without the brightly colored eggs typical of the day. When prepared dye-stuffs are not available, varied colors may be produced by boiling a small quantity of the following with the eggs: for red, Brazil wood; for yellow, Persian berries or a very little turmeric; for brown, a strong dye of turmeric; for a claret color, logwood; for black, logwood and chromate of potash; for blue, a mixture of powdered indigo and crystals of sulphate or iron; for reddish purple, red onion skins.

Common Meats and Game

HEED THESE KEEPING TIMES BEFORE USING PREPARED MEATS:

- Soak all hams 24 hours before cooking.
- Corn beef must remain packed down in salt for 10 or 12 days before being put in brine. It is fit for use after two weeks under the brine.
- Spiced beef must remain three to four weeks in a wooden box or tub, in which it is turned occasionally in the pickle it makes and rubbed with salt.
- Before hanging beef to smoke, it must remain for ten days in the salt, brown sugar, molasses, and saltpeter that has been rubbed on it.
- Allow three weeks to prepare cured beef ham for use; let it remain in molasses a day and two nights and in molasses and salt for

ten additional days; hang it up to dry for one week, then smoke it a little and keep hanging till used.

❧ When the weather will admit of it, mutton is better for being kept a few days before cooking.

❧ Truffle dressing is usually placed in the turkey two days beforehand to impart its flavor to the fowl.

❧ A goose must never be eaten the same day it is killed; if the weather is cold, it should be kept a week before using and before cooking should lie several hours in weak saltwater to remove the strong taste.

❧ Kill young ducks some days before using; or, if obliged to use them the same day as killed, they are better roasted.

Serving Fresh Meat

The faults in the meat generally furnished to us are, first, that it is too new. A beefsteak, which three or four days of keeping might render practicable, is served up to us palpitating with freshness, with all the toughness of animal muscle yet warm.

In the Western country, the traveler, on approaching a hotel, is often saluted by the last shrieks of the chickens which half an hour afterward are presented to him a la spread-eagle for his dinner. The example of the Father of the Faithful, most wholesome to be followed in so many respects, is imitated only in the celerity with which the young calf, tender and good, was transformed into an edible dish for hospitable purposes. But what might be good housekeeping in a nomadic Emir, in days when refrigerators were yet in the future, ought not to be so closely imitated as it often is in our own land.

—Harriet Beecher Stowe, *House and Home Papers,* 1869

ROAST MEAT BEFORE AN OPEN FIRE. Use salt, pepper, butter, or lard, and dredge the meat with flour before roasting, but use little salt at first, as it hardens meat to do otherwise. Baste meat frequently to prevent it from hardening on the outside and to preserve the juices. If possible, roast the meat on a spit before a large, open fire, where there is the intense heat required for cooking and the constantly changing current of air necessary to carry away from the meat the fumes of burning fat, which impair its flavor.

BROIL AS YOU WOULD ROAST. Meat for broiling should be cut from an inch to an inch and a half thick; the surface should be scraped with the back of a knife to remove sawdust and bone dust, and then wiped with a wet cloth but not washed. While the meat is being broiled, heat a dish to receive it; after it is laid upon the hot dish, season it with salt, pepper, and butter on both sides and serve it at once. Broiled meat deteriorates if left standing near the fire any length of time after it is cooked

The introduction of cooking-stoves offers to careless domestics facilities for gradually drying-up meats, and despoiling them of all flavor and nutriment, facilities which appear to be very generally laid hold of. They have almost banished the genuine, old-fashioned roast-meat from our tables, and left in its stead dried meats with their most precious and nutritive juices evaporated. How few cooks, unassisted, are competent to the simple process of broiling a beefsteak or mutton chop! How very generally one has to choose between these meats gradually dried away, or burned on the outside and raw within!

—Harriet Beecher Stowe, *House and Home Papers*, 1869

BAKE MEAT, IF NECESSARY, AT PROPER TEMPERATURES. Baking is not the most desirable way of cooking meat, but ovens are often available when an open fire cannot be reached. It is desirable that the first exposure of meat should be to the greatest obtainable heat, in order to quickly crisp its surface and confine its natural juices.

KEEP MEAT FLAVORING ON HAND. As the housekeeper is sometimes hurried in preparing a dish, it will save time and trouble for her to keep on hand a bottle of meat flavoring compounded by putting in a quart bottle and covering with cider vinegar: 2 chopped onions, 3 pods of red pepper (chopped), 2 tablespoons brown sugar, 1 tablespoon each of celery seed and ground mustard, and 1 teaspoon each of black pepper and salt. A tablespoon of this mixed in a stew, steak, or gravy will impart not only a fine flavor but a rich color.

Pork

SELECT YOUNG PIGS FOR ROASTING. A roasting pig is in prime condition when it is three to six weeks old, with a soft, clean, pinkish white skin, plump hams, a short curly tail, thin delicate ears, and a soft, fringe-like margin all around the tongue.

PREPARE THE PIG FOR ROASTING. As soon as it is killed, plunge it into cold water for five minutes; then rub it all over with powdered resin and put it into scalding water for one minute. Lay it on a clean board and pull and scrape off the bristles, taking care not to injure the skin. When all the bristles are removed, wash the pig thoroughly, first in warm water and then several times in plenty of cold water. Then slit the pig from the throat downward and take out the entrails, laying the heart, liver, lights, and spleen in cold salted water. Wash the pig again in cold water, and wrap it from the air with a cloth wet in cold water until it is wanted for use.

SELECT A TENDER HOG. Hogs weighing from 150 to 200 pounds are the most suitable size for family use. They should not exceed 12 months in age, as they are much more tender from being young, and should have been corn-fed for several weeks.

BUTCHER THE HOG PROPERLY:

🪷 After being properly dressed, hogs should hang long enough to get rid of the animal heat.

▩ When they are ready to be cut up, they should be divided into nine principal parts: two hams, two shoulders, two middlings, the head or face, the jowl, and the chine.

▩ The hog is laid on its back to be cut up.

▩ The head is cut off just below the ears, then it is split down each side of the backbone, which is the chine.

▩ This is divided into three pieces, the upper portion being a choice piece to be eaten cold.

▩ This fat portion may be cut off to make lard.

▩ Each half should then have the loaf fat taken out by cutting the thin skin between it and the ribs.

▩ Just under this, the next thing to be removed is the mousepiece or tenderloin, commencing at the point of the ham. This is considered the most delicate part and is used to make the nicest sausage.

▩ Just under this tenderloin are some short ribs about three inches long, running up from the point of the ham. This portion is removed by a sharp knife being run under it, taking care to cut it smooth and not too thick. When broiled, it is as nice as a partridge.

▩ The ribs are next taken out of the shoulder and middling, though some persons prefer leaving them in the middling; in this case, seven should be taken from the shoulder to make a delicious broil.

▩ Then cut off the ham as near the bone as possible, in a half circle. The shoulder is then cut square across.

▩ The feet are then chopped off with a sharp cleaver. From the shoulder, they should be cut off leaving a stump of about two inches; from the ham, they should be cut off at the joint as smoothly as possible.

SALT THE HAMS. In order to impart redness to the hams, rub on each a teaspoon of pulverized saltpeter before salting. If the weather is very cold, warm the salt before applying it. First, rub and salt the skin side well, and then the fleshy side, using for the purpose a shoe sole or leather glove. No more salt should be used than a sufficiency to preserve the meat, as an excess hardens the meat. A bushel of salt is sufficient for a thousand pounds of meat. For the chine and ribs, a very light sprinkling of salt will suffice.

PACK AND LEAVE THE SALTED MEAT. The meat as salted should be packed with the skin side down, where it should remain from four to six weeks according to the weather. If the weather is mild, four weeks will answer. Should the weather be very cold and the pork in an exposed place, it will freeze; and the salt, failing to penetrate the meat, will be apt to injure it. After it has taken salt sufficiently, it should be hung up for smoking.

Terrapin

Terrapin is distinctive enough to be made a separate course at dinner. Only the flesh, eggs, and liver of terrapin are ordinarily used. Madeira is the proper wine to serve with terrapin.

DRESS IT PROPERLY:

- Loosen the sides of the shells of boiled terrapin, as soon as they are cool enough to handle.

- Lift off the top shell; pull or cut apart the small bands of flesh which hold it to the spine of the terrapin; then rein the under-shell. The entrails of the terrapin have the eggs and liver embedded in them, and the legs are attached to them by crossing bands of flesh.

- Pull off the legs, leaving the flesh attached to them; break off the sharp claws at the extremities of the feet; separate and throw away the head; and put the legs on a dish.

- Carefully remove the eggs and put them into a bowl of hot water.

- Separate the liver from the entrails and cut out that part of the liver which contains the small dark-green gall-bag that can be seen at one side of the liver. The utmost care should taken to avoid cutting or breaking the gall-bag; in removing it, the liver should be held over an empty dish, and if the gall-bag is cut or broken, the liver should be thrown away and the hands washed before the dressing of the terrapin is resumed.

🕸 Cut the liver into half-inch squares and put it with the flesh of the terrapin.

Fish

Fish is a healthful and digestible food. Though not nearly so nutritious as meat, it is considered by many physicians a good brain food, especially if it is broiled.

PRESERVE LIVING FISH. Stop their mouths up with crumbs of bread steeped in brandy, pour a very small quantity of brandy into them, and pack them in clean straw. In this way, it is said fish may be preserved in a torpid state for 12 or 15 days, and when put into water will come to life again after three or four hours.

CLEAN AGAIN AT HOME. Although fish should be cleaned at the market, one should not trust entirely to such cleaning, but pass the edge of the knife over the fish to remove any remaining scales. Wash it inside and out with a wet cloth, and dry carefully with a towel. Rub it next with salt and pepper and lay it on a dish or hang it up till you are ready to cook. Never keep it lying in water, either in preparing it for cooking or in trying to keep it till the next day.

Fish larded and baked

The Frenchman, who locks the door of his shop from half-past twelve till two o'clock, so as not to be disturbed by customers while he is having his dinner with his wife, and a good time with the children, I say, this man has solved the great problem, the only problem of life, happiness, far better than the American who, at one o'clock, will stick at his door: "Gone to dinner; shall be back in five minutes." Five minutes to dinner, just think of it! The greatest event of the day. And what is the result of that five minutes to dinner in America? The result is that the whole continent, from New York to San Francisco, from British Columbia to Louisiana, cities, forests, prairies, the whole landscape, is spoiled, made an eyesore of, by the advertisements of liver pills.

—"Studies in Cheerfulness–1," 1898

Cook fish one of these four ways:

Before boiling, rub fish carefully with a little vinegar. Boil in salted boiling water, with one tablespoon vinegar, allowing ten minutes to a pound. Try with a needle; if it runs through easily, the fish is done. It will require an hour to boil a large fish and about 20 minutes for a small one.

Be careful to have boiling hot lard in the frying pan when you go to fry fish. First rub salt and pepper and flour or meal on the fish, then keep it covered while frying until it reaches a pretty amber color.

Fish which are either watery or very oily are best when cooked with direct exposure to the fire. Before broiling, rub with pepper and salt and then grease with fresh butter. Lay the fish on a gridiron well greased with sweet lard and lay the tin sheet over it. When you wish to turn, take the gridiron from the fire, holding the tin sheet on top of the fish; hold them together, lay them on a table with the tin sheet down and the gridiron uppermost, raise the gridiron, and easily slide the fish onto it to put it again on the fire and brown the other side, putting the tin sheet back on top of it. When done, lay the fish on a dish and pour sauce over it.

🌣 Gash fish for baking straight across—a half-inch deep, two inches long, and one inch apart—and lay in strips of pork. Place in pan and cover the bottom with water a half-inch deep; add one teaspoon of butter and one tablespoon of salt. Dredge fish with flour and baste often. Keep up your supply of gravy as it boils away. Try with a knitting needle and take up with a cake turner.

🌣 To lard fish for baking, remove a large piece of the skin from the back of the fish and insert the lardoon. The lardoons are protected by buttered paper until the fish is nearly done; then the paper is removed to permit them to brown.

PREPARE SAUCES FOR SOME FISH. The very dry-fleshed fish should be served with a sauce. Whitefish have far less oil distributed through their bodies and are therefore not so rich as darker-colored fish, and need richer sauces and dressings. In making sauces for fish, never use the water in which the fish has been boiled. Larded fish is generally stuffed and served with a brown mushroom sauce.

Vegetables

Every food that has grown in the ground is called a vegetable. Not until they are growing near where we live can we expect to find them cheap. During the summer, if you can get them fresh and cook them nicely, you will not need to buy nearly as much meat and can make many nice dishes, mostly all vegetables.

BOIL OR DRY CORN. Cold-boiled corn, cut from the ear and mixed with an equal quantity of cold potatoes chopped, can be fried with salt, pepper, and butter or heated with cold stewed tomatoes and served on toast. Or, cut the grains from ears of tender corn, spread them on large sheets of paper in the sun, and dry them thoroughly; or put them on pans in a cool oven and dry them. After the corn is dried, keep it in a cool, dry place. When it is wanted for the table, soak it overnight in enough water or milk to cover it; the next day boil it tender in the same water, season it with salt, pepper, and butter, and serve it hot.

PICK AND SOAK ROOTS. Roots, including carrots, oyster-plants, beets, potatoes, and parsnips, are mostly vegetables that will last all winter if properly taken care of. Toward spring, you must pick off the sprouts, lest they become rank; soak them to plump them and cook them with greater care. The roots are particularly nice when they first come, if quite ripe. When young and tender, they require less time to cook.

DON'T ADD COLD MILK FOR MASHING POTATOES. Mashed potatoes will be hard, sticky, and heavy if you turn cold milk upon them while they are steaming hot; by adding scalding milk and beating them thoroughly, they will be light and feathery. Until served, they should be covered close with a napkin.

USE SCALDING OIL FOR FRYING POTATOES. Fried potatoes will be soaked and leathery if the fat is not hot enough and if they are not well drained when taken out.

USE SALT FOR SOME, SUGAR FOR OTHERS. Asparagus and celery are both cooked as a vegetable and seasoned with butter and salt, but rhubarb, which is more for a sauce, has only sugar cooked in it.

PRESERVE TOMATOES FOR WINTER. Take the tomatoes when perfectly ripe and scald them in hot water in order to take off the skin easily. When skinned, boil them well in a little sugar or salt but no water. Then spread them in cakes about an inch thick and place the cakes in the sun. They will, in three or four days, be sufficiently dried to pack away in bags, which should hang in a dry place.

PROCURE PLENTY OF SPINACH. In respect to quantity, spinach is desperately deceitful. I never see it drained after it is boiled without thinking of a young housekeeper who purchased a quart of spinach and ordered a spring dinner for herself and husband. When it should have appeared upon the table, there came in its stead a platter of sliced egg, she having given out one for the dressing. "Where is the spinach?" she demanded of the maid. "Under the egg, ma'am!" And it was really all there. The moral: Get enough spinach to be visible to the naked eye. A peck is not too much for a family of four or five.

Seasonings

A man is able to work longer and better if his meals are nourishing. He does not know when to add salt or pepper, and why should he? It should be the care of the wife or daughter to so season the food that the first mouthful is appetizing.

PREPARE A BOUQUET OF HERBS FOR FLAVOR. Hold a small bunch of parsley in the left palm; lay on it a small stalk of celery, a bay leaf, a sprig of any sweet herb except sage, a blade of mace, and a dozen peppercorns or a small red-pepper pod; fold the parsley so as to enclose all the other seasonings and tie it in a compact little bundle. This is called a bouquet, or fagot, of herbs, in French cookbooks, and serves to give an indescribable and delicious flavor to the dishes in which it is cooked.

Relishes

The innumerable small appetizers known as relishes, or hors d'oeuvres, include all forms of pickles and table sauces, small sandwiches and crusts garnished with highly seasoned meats, various preparations of cheese and eggs; in short, any small, highly spiced or seasoned dish calculated to rouse or stimulate the appetite.

CONSIDER THESE RELISHES:

☞ *Smoked Fish.* Small strips of cured fish, either salted or smoked, are acceptable as a relish; or small fish which have been preserved in oil, such as anchovies or sardines, may be wiped dry with a towel and served with vinegar or lemon juice. Smoked eels, herring, halibut, sturgeon, tunny-fish, salt cod, salmon, Finnan haddie, Yarmouth bloaters, or any dried fish may be served; only it must be delicately prepared in small pieces and with some suitable garnish, so as to be an appreciable incentive to the enjoyment of the heavier dishes which succeed it. Sliced lemon is always a good garnish for any highly seasoned relish.

☞ *Sandwich Butter.* Mix together equal parts good butter and grated ham or tongue; season rather highly with salt, cayenne, and mustard mixed with vinegar. Pack the mixture into little earthen jars; cover each jar with a piece of paper dipped in brandy and then exclude the air by a tight cover or a bladder wet and then tied over the top; keep in a cool, dry place. The flavor may be changed by varying the ingredients and seasoning.

☞ *Sandwiches.* Very acceptable sandwiches can be made with the potted and devilled meats and game now sold in jars and tins. The bread should be quite free from crust, cut in thin small slices, and thinly spread with the best butter. A thin layer of highly seasoned meat, game, poultry, or some kind of spiced or salted fish is put between two slices of buttered bread, irregular edges are trimmed off, and the sandwiches kept cool until served.

☞ *Canapés.* Canapés are small slices of bread slightly hollowed out on the upper surface and then fried golden brown in plenty of smoking hot fat. The little hollow is filled with any highly seasoned meat and the canapés served either hot or cold.

☞ *Puff-pastes.* Puff-pastes are forms of pastry made both in sweets and with delicate force-meats and ragouts to be served as hot entrées. Timbales are small patties baked in deep, smooth moulds. Bouchees are very small shells of puff-paste filled with any highly seasoned mince or ragout and served both hot and cold. Rissoles, the smallest puff-paste, are turnovers filled with highly seasoned mince and either baked or fried like croquettes.

CONSIDER PICKLES AS RELISHES AND HEED THESE PICKLING TIMES:

❦ Oysters must stand two days covered in stewed juice and vinegar to become pickled.

❦ Pickle vinegar ought to be prepared several months before using and always kept on hand ready for use.

❦ Three weeks is long enough for green pickles to remain in brine, if you wish to make your pickle early in the fall.

❦ Yellow pickle must stand for two 24-hour periods in brine, poured over while hot; on the third day, spread them on a board or table and let them stand in the hot sun four days, taking care that no dew shall fall on them.

❦ For boiled cucumber pickle, take fresh cucumbers, put them in brine for a few days, then take them out and put them in vinegar to soak for two days.

❦ Sweet tomato pickle will be ready for use in a fortnight after being prepared, poured into a stone jar, and sealed tight.

❦ Mangoes must have been in brine two weeks and greened, as you would cucumbers, before being stuffed and covered with vinegar in a jar to be stored.

❦ Pepper mangoes must be packed closely in a stone jar (with the small end downwards) in vinegar for three weeks to be ready for use.

❦ Walnuts to be pickled remain in saltwater for five or six weeks, then in fresh water for 24 hours, and are ready for use in two or three weeks.

❦ Keep martinas covered in very strong brine for ten days, then wash and put them in vinegar to stand ten more days before putting them in the jar intended for them.

❦ For chow-chow, pack ingredients in salt for a night, soak in vinegar and water for two days, and boil for three mornings.

Desserts

SELECT DESSERTS BY THE DINNER. When you have a hearty, salt-meat dinner, use a cold, light, delicate pudding, like a boiled custard. When you have a fish dinner, which does not give the nourishment that meat does, serve a boiled, hearty pudding. A lemon cornstarch pudding can be used when you are short of milk, and a broken cold pudding can be made fresh again by arranging it in a clean dish and covering it with a meringue.

HEAT THE OVEN PROPERLY FOR CAKES. A layer of sand on the bottom of the oven, about half an inch thick, is a safeguard against burning on the bottom. If the general heat is too great, the cake will burn or crack on the top before it can bake properly; if the oven is not hot enough, the cake will not rise properly. A safe test of the heat is to put a spoon of the cake dough or batter on a bit of buttered paper and slip it into the oven; if the little cake bakes evenly and quickly without burning at the edge, the heat is right.

BAKE DEEP CAKES WITH PAPER. When a cake pan is too shallow for the quantity of cake desired, extend it with stiff glazed paper thickly coated with butter; if the oven heat is moderate, the butter will preserve the paper from burning.

HAVE LIGHTNESS IN MIND WHEN BAKING. Whoever eats heavy pie crust commits a crime against his physical well-being and must pay the penalty. The good housewife should see to it that all pastry and cakes are light; no others should be eaten.

USE A FREEZER TO MAKE ICE CREAM. The old way of freezing cream consisted of occasionally stirring the cream while it was freezing in a tin can set in a tub of ice and salt. A more easy and expeditious method is the patent freezer. The principle underlying all the best-known patents is the mixing of the cream by a wooden beater which revolves inside the can by the same motion that slightly changes the position of the can in the outer tub of ice and salt.

TAKE CARE IN PREPARING THE ICE-CREAM MIXTURE. Ice creams of the most ordinary sort are made of milk thickened with arrowroot or cornstarch in the proportion of a tablespoon to a quart, dissolved in cold water, and boiled in the milk, which is cooled, sweetened, and flavored before it is frozen. The freezing mixture should be composed of three parts of crushed ice to one of coarse salt, and care should be taken that it does not reach high enough around the sides of the can to penetrate to the interior and so spoil the cream.

COLOR THE CREAM IF YOU WISH. Boil very slowly in a gill of water, till reduced to half, 20 grains of cochineal and the same of alum and finely powdered cream of tartar; strain and keep in a phial. For yellow coloring, use an infusion of saffron; for green, use spinach leaves boiled and the juice expressed; for red, express juice from the pokeberry. To every pint allow a pound of sugar and boil 15 minutes. A teaspoon of this jelly will color two quarts of milk.

SET AWAY PLUM PUDDING FOR THE MORROW. To keep plum puddings good for some months, hang them in a cold place in the cloth in which they are boiled. When wanted, take them out of the cloth, cover them with a clean one, and warm them through with hot water.

Introduction of Dr. Price's Harmless Food Colors

There has never been a time like the present, when housekeepers gave so much attention to the apperance as well as to the palatableness of household cookery {...} A love of daintiness is inherent in the heart of every true housewife, and when this can be gained without loss of health or comfort, a great boon has been conferred.

Color schemes enter largely into all forms of entertainment today, and in order to meet these requirements, a fine line of exquisitely prepared liquid colors has been placed on the market by Dr. Price {...} to be used fearlessly to color cake, frostings, ices, sherbets, and creams.

LIST OF COLORS:
FRUIT COLORING, STRAWBERRY RED, LEMON YELLOW, CHOCOLATE BROWN, PURPLE VIOLET, BLOOD ORANGE, APPLE GREEN

—*Dr. Price's Delicious Desserts*, 1904

Daily Cooking Tasks

Every moment has its appointed duty, and one neglected never comes back to give us a new trial.

AT SUNRISE:

- Kill the turtle in summer for turtle soup and hang it up to bleed.
- Sift flour for plum pudding; in winter, set it in a warm place; in summer, set it in a cool pace to rise.

BEFORE BREAKFAST:

- Always shape and put bread in the molds.
- Always try to make cake before breakfast or as early in the morning as possible.
- Begin preparing vegetable soup for dinner, if served at two o'clock.

IN THE COOL OF THE MORNING:

- Try to churn, as fewer flies are swarming then, and the butter can be made much firmer.
- Also, print butter, make pastry, and gather vegetables.
- If you are living in the city, get your vegetables from market as early in the morning as possible.

AFTER BREAKFAST:

- Make leaven in winter.
- Set dough to rise at eleven o'clock in the morning for early tea.
- Blanch Jordan almonds that have been soaked overnight for cheesecakes, using cold water; lay them on a clean cloth to dry, then beat them fine in a marble mortar with a little orange-flower or rose water.
- In cool weather, make fritters about nine o'clock in the morning; in summer, about eleven o'clock.

- Make ice cream early in the day and set it aside, leaving more leisure for other preparations that are better made immediately before dinner.
- Begin preparing stewed chicken for dinner immediately after breakfast.
- Begin cooking corned beef-tongue for dinner; put the beef on in a large pot of water early in the morning and simmer for hours.
- Make up yeast in the morning; it ought to be fit for use at night.
- Sun and air flour, whether old or new, before using; in the morning, get out the flour to be made up at night for next morning's breakfast, sift it in a tray, and put it out in the sun; or, if the day is damp, set it near the kitchen fire.

IN THE EVENING:
- Send the children to gather vegetables, as well as cut flowers, to garnish cold meats and salads for the next day's dinner.
- Pick fully ripe figs for fig preserves and let them soak all night in very weak salt water.
- Set dried peas to soak overnight; hominy in hot water to boil the next day; ham the night before you wish to boil it; salt pork in skimmed milk to bake like fresh pork for salt pork almost as good as fresh roast pork; ingredients for liver pudding (hog's heads, livers, lights, milts, sweetbreads, kidneys) together in a tub of salt and water; Jordan almonds in cold water for almond cheesecake; tapioca in a little water for tapioca cream.
- Prepare the fruit for fruit cake the day before
- Kill the chicken the day before broiling.

Seasonal Tasks

IN SUMMER:
- In May, make pickle vinegar, which should sun all summer.

- Kill and dress the poultry the day beforehand, except chicken for frying, which is not good unless killed the same day it is eaten.
- It is best to use five teacups of flour, instead of four, when making pastry.
- Make bread dough with cold water; apply no artificial heat to it, but set it in a cool place to ferment.

IN FALL:

- Bottle currant wine in September.
- Late as possible in the fall prepare tender roasting ears for winter use.
- In cool weather, set dough before the fire, both before and after making it into rolls.
- In October and November, engage butter to be brought weekly, fresh from the churn in rolls.

IN WINTER:

- Corned beef prepared in January will keep well through the month of March, improving with the lapse of time.
- Put beef and tongue about the middle of February in brine; rub first with salt and let them lie for a fortnight, then throw them in brine and let them lay there three weeks before hanging in a cool, dark place.
- A smothered fire for curing bacon should be made up three times a day till the middle of March or first of April.
- Make bread dough with lukewarm water in winter; make it up at seven o' clock, then set it on a shelf under which a lighted coal-oil lamp is placed. Set yeast in a warm place in the winter to ferment.
- It is well to keep soup stock on hand in cold weather, as by the addition of a can of tomatoes or other ingredients, a delicious soup may be quickly made of it.

IN SPRING:

- Draw off crab cider in March, and it is fit for use.
- In curing bacon, the joint pieces should be taken down in the middle of March or first of April and packed in hickory or other green-wood ashes, as in salt, where they will remain all summer without danger of bugs interfering with them.
- In curing hams, on the first of April, take them down and pack in coal ashes or pine ashes well slaked.
- It is best to scald the vinegar in the spring when making oil mangoes.
- The liquid for yellow pickle vinegar should be spiced in the spring and set in the sun until autumn.

Measurements

HOUSEHOLD MEASURES FOR SOLID INGREDIENTS INCLUDE:

Wheat flour	1 pound is 1 quart.
Indian meal	1 pound 2 ounces are 1 quart.
Butter	When soft, 1 pound is 1 pint.
Loaf sugar	Broken, 1 pound is 1 quart.
Powdered white sugar	1 pound 1 ounce are 1 quart.
Best brown sugar	1 pound 2 ounces are 1 quart.
Eggs	10 eggs are 1 pound.
Flour	8 quarts are 1 peck; 4 pecks are 1 bushel.

HOUSEHOLD MEASURES FOR LIQUID INGREDIENTS INCLUDE:

- 1 tablespoon is ½ ounce.
- 60 drops are equal to 1 teaspoon.
- 4 teaspoons are equal to 1 tablespoon
- 16 large tablespoons are ½ pint.
- 8 large tablespoons are 1 gill.
- 2 gills are ½ pint.
- A common sized tumbler holds ½ pint.

Cook's Measures Include:

- Use a piece the size of a walnut.
- Make it up into balls the size of an orange.
- Use a lump the size of a hen's egg/a guinea egg/a turkey's egg.
- Use a lump the size of a thimble.
- Use a handful.
- Cut in pieces the size of your hand.
- Use a lump as large as your double fist.
- Pat into pones as wide as the wrist.
- Use a pinch.
- Cut in tolerably thick slices.
- Use a heaping plateful.
- Use the weight of 12 eggs.
- Use enough to make a batter the consistency of sponge cake batter.
- Add brandy, as much as you think best.

The Best Cook's Measure for Doneness Is Amber.

- Keep covered everything that is being fried. Doing this will enable you to fry articles of food *a pretty amber color*, while at the same time it will be perfectly done.
- For example, when frying chicken, cover closely and fry *till a fine amber color.*
- When roasting turkey, baste and turn frequently *till every part is a beautiful brown amber color.*
- In baking bread, *when the top of the loaf is a light amber color,* put back the paper that the bread may not brown too much while thoroughly baking.
- The *palest amber jelly,* clear and sparkling, flavored only by the grated rind and juice of a lemon and pale Madeira or sherry wine, is not only the most beautiful, but the most palatable jelly that can be made.
- When making tomato preserves, take the boiled tomatoes out *when they become amber-colored.*

- In making peach preserves, when all the peaches have been boiled and set in the sun, put back the first dish of peaches in the kettle, *taking them out when a pretty amber color,* and so on till all have been boiled twice.

Chapter Twelve

For the Daily Cook: Family Table Recipes for Breakfast, Luncheon, and Supper

BREAD AND CEREALS

Spoonbread

2 cups sweet milk
2 cups buttermilk
4 eggs
1 tablespoon butter, melted
4 tablespoons flour
2 cups cornmeal
1 teaspoon soda

Beat eggs lightly. Add sweet milk, buttermilk, and butter. Combine cornmeal, flour, and soda and add to liquid mixture. Bake at 375 degrees for 35–40 minutes in a greased dish. Mrs. Jenkins said this is good!

—Mrs. Robert F. Jenkins, Amarillo, Texas
First Baptist Church Cookbook, 1909

Breakfast Menus

Plums and Pears

Corn Meal Mush

Baked Beans   Fish Balls   Brown Bread

Coffee

Peaches

Farinose with Sugar and Cream

Omelet   Potatoes à la Maître d'Hôtel   Cream Muffins

Coffee

—*The Boston Cooking-School Cook Book,* 1896

Corn Meal Mush

Have a kettle of fresh boiling water. Sift a cup of cornmeal into a saucepan, add a teaspoon of salt, and cold water enough to moisten. Pour in a little hot water, stir until smooth, set on the stove, and pour in about a quart of boiling water. Stir constantly until it boils, then cover and set back where it will cook moderately until well done. If

Inexorably Sam Galloway saddled his pony. He was going away from the Rancho Altito at the end of a three-months' visit. It is not to be expected that a guest should put up with wheat coffee and biscuits yellow-streaked with saleratus for longer than that.

—"Last of the Troubadours,"
July 1908

necessary, pour in a little more boiling water. Don't scorch. Serve with milk or butter.

—*The Capitol Cook Book,* 1899

Potato Yeast Bread

Sift flour into a pan or bowl, make a hollow in the middle, and drop in your salt and sugar. Stir in yeast and add milk and warm water enough to form a stiff batter. Let it rise, then knead in as much flour as it will take; set it to rise again. Mold it into loaves, and when it is light enough, bake in a moderate oven.

—Mrs. Dixon Lewers, Palestine, Texas
The First Texas Cookbook, 1883

Sally Lunn

    1 pint flour
    2 tablespoons sugar
    salt
    1 cup milk
    2 tablespoons Cottonlene
    ½ cake compressed yeast
    1 egg

Sift together flour, sugar, and a little salt. Warm milk and melt in Cottonlene. Stir into the flour, adding also the compressed yeast dissolved in a little lukewarm water. Beat very well and add egg, yolk and white beaten separately. Pour all into buttered cake pan and let rise until double its bulk, about 2 hours. Sprinkle lightly with granulated sugar and bake in a moderately hot oven. Cut into squares and serve warm.

—*Home Helps,* 1910

Breakfast Tea

Of late, the introduction of English breakfast tea has raised a new sect among the tea-drinkers, reversing some of the old canons. Breakfast tea must be boiled! Unlike the delicate article of olden time, which required only a momentary infusion to develop its richness, this requires a longer and severer treatment to bring out its strength—thus confusing all the established usages, and throwing the work into the hands of the cook in the kitchen. The faults of tea, as too commonly found at our hotels and boarding houses, are that it is made in every way the reverse of what it should be. The water is hot, perhaps, but not boiling; the tea has a general flat, stale, smoky taste, devoid of life or spirit; and it is served, usually, with thin milk, instead of cream. Cream is as essential to the richness of tea as of coffee.

—*House and Home Papers*, 1869

Cream Fritters

   1 pint milk
   1 pint Quaker Oats
   ½ cup sugar
   teaspoon vanilla
   eggs
   bread crumbs
   powdered sugar

Put into a double boiler milk and Quaker Oats; stir until each grain is moistened with milk; cover the kettle and cook slowly for 1 hour. Add sugar and vanilla and turn into a square pan to cool. When cold, cut into strips the length of your finger and one inch wide. Dip in egg and then in bread crumbs and fry in smoking hot fat. Drain on brown paper, dust with powdered sugar, and serve hot.

—*Cereal Foods and How to Cook Them*, 1899

> "*Too* much enthusiasm and chattering at breakfast are like too much red at sunrise," the doctor always said; "a dull, bad day follows it."
>
> —*Remember the Alamo*, 1898

Popovers

2 large or 3 small eggs
2 cups flour
½ teaspoon salt
2 cups milk

Beat eggs well; mix carefully flour, salt, and eggs. Pour into hot greased irons and bake in hot oven a ½ hour or more, according to size. Serve promptly.

—*Home Helps*, 1910

Excellent Light Biscuits

4 large Irish potatoes
Egg-sized piece of lard
1 teacup milk
1 teacup yeast
2 quarts flour

Boil potatoes. While hot, mash them with lard. Add milk and yeast. Stir in enough flour to make a good batter (about 2 quarts) and set to rise. When light, make up the dough. You generally have to add more water or milk. Roll thick and let them rise slowly, but bake them quickly.

—*Miss Corson's Practical American Cookery and Household Management*, 1885

Grandpa's Favorite Griddle Cakes

3 eggs
1 quart milk
2 cups stale bread crumbs
1 tablespoon melted butter
1 teaspoon salt
flour

Beat eggs well. Mix milk and stale bread crumbs. Work until smooth, stir in melted butter and eggs, then add salt. Lastly add just enough flour to bind the mixture. If too thick, add milk. These are wholesome and good. Take care they do not stick to the griddle.

—*Common Sense in the Household*, 1871

Fried Bread (or Egg Toast)

    stale bread
    1 egg
    1 pint milk
    pinch of salt
    1 teaspoon sugar
    1 teaspoon flour

Cut bread ¼ inch thick. Beat eggs and smooth in a little of the milk (allow one egg to each pint of milk) and put together with salt, sugar, and flour. Soak six slices of a loaf, turning them over in milk. Put a little sweet lard on the griddle and fry each slice to a delicate brown on both sides. Use the pancake turner. Some like a little cinnamon sprinkled on when taken up. Pile up, keep hot, and serve—it's good. Make egg toast the same way but without the flour or sugar.

Crackling Bread

    1 pint meal
    salt
    1–2 cups cracklings

Chop cracklings rather fine and soften with 1 cup hot water. Pour water off cracklings and use it to scald the meal and salt, just enough to dampen. Add cracklings and cold water to make thick batter. Dip your hands in cold water and mold the bread into pones and place in piping hot greased pan. Bake on top shelf of quick oven.

Uses for Stale Bread

- **STALE BREAD BATTER CAKES.** Put a loaf of stale bread to stand all day in a pint of milk. Just before tea, add 3 eggs and 1 large spoonful of butter. If too thin, add a little flour.

- **BREADING.** Stale bread may be laid aside until thoroughly dried, then rolled very fine. Put this into a wide-mouthed bottle into which you can dip a spoon. This is useful in many ways, as in breading veal chops or oysters.

- **WATER TOAST.** The bread should be nicely browned, then dipped quickly in salted water. Do not spread butter over it, but place little bits to melt; this prevents the toast from being broken.

- **QUEEN TOAST.** Queen toast is made by soaking the slices in a very plain uncooked custard and browning them in a frying pan. When serving, sprinkle sugar and cinnamon between the slices as they are piled upon the dish.

- **TOAST CRUMBS.** Toast crumbs are made of buttered bread cut in very small cubes and placed in the oven to brown. These are nice served with soup.

—*The Cooking Garden*, 1885

Crullers

5 eggs
½ teacup brown sugar
2 tablespoons sweet milk
1 teaspoon butter
1 teaspoon cinnamon
2 teaspoons yeast powder

Have a great deal of hot lard in the spider; use enough flour to make a soft dough. Cut in thick squares and fry.

—Miss Julia Crow, Austin, Texas
The First Texas Cookbook, 1883

The Most Economical Breakfast Dish (beautiful also)

Keep a jar for remnants of bread, both coarse and fine, potatoes, remnants of hominy, rice, grits, cracked wheat, oatmeal, and all other articles used on the table. Add all remnants of milk, whether sour or sweet, and water enough to soak all, so as to be soft, but not thin. When enough is collected, add enough water to make a batter for griddle cakes and put in enough soda to sweeten it. Add 2 spoons of sugar, ½ a teaspoon of salt, and 2 eggs for each quart, and you make an excellent dish of material, most of it usually wasted. Thicken it a little with fine flour, and it makes fine waffles.

—*Miss Beecher's Housekeeper and Healthkeeper*, 1873

Pearl Wheat or Cracked Wheat

Boil one pint in a pail set in boiling water until quite soft, but so as not to lose its form. Add a teaspoon each of sugar and salt; also add water, when needed. It must boil a long time. Each a part for supper, with sugar and cream, and the next morning add 2 eggs, a great spoonful of sugar, and fine flour enough to make it suitable for muffin rings or drop cakes.

—*Miss Beecher's Housekeeper and Healthkeeper*, 1873

MEAT STUFFS

Chili Con Carne with Frijoles

Heat lard in a covered pot. Chop cold roast or soup meat and add salt and 1 tablespoon flour. Cook a while then add a cup of hot water and 1 tablespoon chili powder. Boil until meat is tender and serve with frijoles.

Scrappel

Boil a hog's head and let it stand 5–6 hours or all night. Slip out the bones and chop finely; then return the meat to the liquor. Skim when first cold; warm and season freely with pepper, salt, sage, and sweet herbs. Add 2 cups buckwheat meal and 1 cup cornmeal. Put into molds and, when cold, cut into slices and fry for breakfast.

—*Mrs. Winslow's Domestic Receipt Book,* 1877

Veal Loaf

> 3 pounds raw veal
> 1 heaping teaspoon each of salt and pepper
> 2 raw eggs
> cracker crumbs
> melted butter

Finely chop raw veal and mix together with salt and pepper, raw eggs, and about 2 tablespoons water. Mold this into a loaf, then roll it in cracker crumbs, and pour melted butter over it. Place it in a pan and bake 2 hours. Slice off when cold.

—*Mrs. Winslow's Domestic Receipt Book,* 1877

Luncheon Menus

Turkey Soup   Veal Loaf   Lettuce Salad
Bavarian Cream

Bouillon   Deviled Clams
Lettuce Sandwiches   Chicken à la Terrapin
Peach Sherbet

—The Enterprising Housekeeper, 1898

Beef Stew with Dumplings
Sliced Oranges   Cake   Tea

Lobster Salad   Rolls
Raspberries and Cream   Wafers   Russian Tea

—The Boston Cooking-School Cook Book, 1896

Tamale Pie

>   dressed chicken
>   butter or sweet lard
>   1 can tomatoes
>   1 large onion

2 chili peppers
salt
about a dozen olives
6 hard-boiled eggs
pie crust

Take a dressed chicken and cut up into small pieces. Put butter or sweet lard in the bottom of a pot, place chicken in, and brown nicely. Add tomatoes, onion, chili peppers, a little salt, and hot water; stew until tender. Thicken gravy and turn all into a deep earthen dish. Drop olives through the stew and slice hard-boiled eggs over the top. Cover all with a rich pie crust, put in the oven, and bake.

—Mrs. Conway, *The Capitol Cook Book*, 1899

Fricandelles

Take meat—the more variety the better—hash it finely and mix with 2 eggs, grated onion, melted butter, pounded crackers, pepper, and salt. Form into balls and fry in butter. Serve with drawn butter flavored with lemon. Salt Rheum is cured by Hood's Sarsaparilla.

—*Hood's Cook Book Reprint Number One*, 1877

Salmon Croquettes

Mix together 1 can of salmon, a pint of mashed Irish potatoes, 2 eggs, a tablespoon of butter and salt and pepper and mold all in a shape you desire before frying in boiling grease to a golden color. Insert cloves in the ends of each patty for a nice luncheon dish.

Barbecued Fish

Salt the fish, put in a baking pan, cover with boiling water, boil slowly until almost done, then pour off nearly all the water. Add a sauce made of a cup of vinegar, a tablespoon of butter, ½ teaspoon black pepper, and a little Worcester sauce; baste until well done and nicely brown.

—*The Capitol Cook Book*, 1899

At 2 p.m. lunch

I commonly invite to that—cup of tea and biscuit and butter with cold meat—any gentleman I wish to have more conference with than is practicable in hours given to miscellaneous business.

—President Rutherford B. Hayes,
White House Diary, March 18, 1878

Oyster Pie

Line a baking dish with a rich paste. Put in a layer of oysters (canned are just as good as fresh) with salt and pepper. Then add a layer of sliced or chopped hard-boiled eggs. Season with more salt and pepper and small lumps of butter. Add another layer of oysters, then eggs until the dish is nearly full. Pour in oyster liquor, cover with pastry, and cut a cross in the center. A few minutes before done, add a little sweet milk. Brown and serve hot.

—Mrs. Sue E. Vannoy, *The Capitol Cook Book*, 1899

Hamburg Steak for Breakfast or Supper

Remove bone and gristle from 1 pound of steak and grind the steak in a meat chopper. Heat 2 spoons of butter in a frying pan, and, when hot, put in the chopped meat. Sift a little flour over it and pepper and salt. When the meat is cooked, add 1 cup milk and a ½ cup hot water, stirring all the while. Let this boil up and then pour it over buttered toast.

Jerked Beef for Lunch

Our lunch consisted of . . . of . . . well, a yard or so of jerked beef and some cool spring water. The approved Texan mode of eating this dried beef is as follows: you insert the end firmly between the teeth . . . apply the knife close to the lips, and then cut and pull. If the other end flies across, and is likely to strike your neighbor's face, he must dodge. I see not how else the matter is to be arranged.

—"Solid Days in Texas," June 1871

VEGETABLES, TOO

Many of these dishes will serve you just as well at breakfast, luncheon, supper, or dinner.

Macaroni Casserole

½ pound macaroni
½ pound sliced American or Canadian cheese
¼ pound diced bacon
½ can tomatoes or 4 fresh sliced tomatoes
1½ teaspoons salt
⅛ teaspoon pepper

Boil the macaroni for an hour. Drain and mix with the other ingredients. Put in a casserole oiled with bacon fat and add a little milk or water if the mixture seems dry. Cover and bake in a slow oven until done.

—*Cook Book: "New Process" Wick Oil Cook Stove*, circa 1910

Frijoles

Soak a pint of beans over night in weak soda water. Boil the next morning in fresh water, with salt and some lard or bacon, until tender. For another dish, take cold frijoles, mash them smooth, and spread them in a baking dish. Cover with butter and brown nicely.

Olla Podrida

   1 small onion
   1 tablespoon butter
   1 pint green corn
   1 pint okra
   1 pint butter beans
   1 pint tomatoes
   black and red pepper
   and salt to taste
   chopped chicken or beef (optional)

Luncheon, as the mid-day meal in the ordinary household, is far too often an indifferent affair... Luncheon is, in many places, peculiarly the woman's meal, and for this very reason sufficient care and thought should be expended upon it to tempt the delicate appetite and give the needed nourishment in an attractive form.

Relishes are nowhere more acceptable than upon the luncheon table, but that which deserves the highest consideration for this meal is the utilization of culinary odds and ends. Croquettes, soufflés, meats for sandwiches, and all meat entrees become simplified by means of a meat chopper, and the majority of dishes coming under the head of entrees are but different forms of hash or minced meat.

—*The Enterprising Housekeeper*, 1898

Fry finely chopped onion in butter until light brown; add green corn, okra, butter beans, tomatoes, and enough water to cook tender. Add gravy if preferred. Season highly with black and red pepper and salt. If desired, add finely chopped chicken or beef.

—Mrs. Charles D. Walsh, *The Capitol Cook Book*, 1899

Broiled Tomatoes

Wipe, scald, peel, and cut tomatoes in halves; lay on a wire broiler; and when hot add a bit of butter, pepper, and salt. Serve when brown. Or, sprinkle tomatoes with buttered crumbs before broiling.

—*Home Helps*, 1910

Supper Menus

Shrimp Salad   Saratoga Potatoes
Brown Bread and Butter Sandwiches   Coffee
Lemon Jelly   Wafers

Steamed Clams, Butter Sauce
Veal Loaf   Spiced Currants
Cake   Iced Tea   Orange Sherbet

Broiled Tomatoes   Potato Croquettes
Peach Shortcake   Chocolate

—*The Enterprising Housekeeper*, 1898

Saratoga Potatoes

Peel and slice thin the potatoes and place in cold water. Drain well and dry in a towel. Fry a few at a time in hot Cottolene. Salt as you take them out and lay them on coarse brown paper for a short time. They are very nice cold for lunch or to take to picnics.

—*Home Helps*, 1910

Corn and Cheese Soufflé

    1 tablespoon butter
    1 tablespoon chopped green pepper
    ¼ cup flour
    2 cups milk
    1 cup chopped corn
    1 cup grated cheese
    3 eggs
    ½ teaspoon salt

Melt the butter and cook the pepper thoroughly in it. Make a sauce out of the flour, milk, and cheese; add the corn, egg yolks, and salt. Cut and fold in the egg whites beaten stiffly; turn into a buttered baking dish and bake over a medium flame 30 minutes.

—*Cook Book: "New Process" Wick Oil Cook Stove*, circa 1910

Potatoes à la Maître d'Hôtel

    1 pint potato balls
    ½ pint milk
    1 egg
    2 tablespoons butter
    1 tablespoon lemon juice
    1 tablespoon minced parsley
    ½ teaspoon salt
    1 pinch paprika

Boil potato balls in salted water about 10 minutes, drain, and cut with a vegetable cutter. Pour hot milk over them. When the milk is partly absorbed, quickly stir in 1 egg yolk, beaten to a cream, with the butter, lemon juice, parsley, salt, and paprika. Serve as soon as sauce thickens.

—*Home Helps*, 1910

Mock Oysters

    1 cup cooked and mashed parsnips
    egg
    4 soda crackers rolled fine
    2 tablespoons cream
    ½ teaspoon salt
    ½ teaspoon pepper
    1 teaspoon Worcestershire sauce or catsup

Add liquids and seasonings to parsnips, then egg and crackers. Let stand 30 minutes, then form into oyster-shaped patties and dip patties in slightly beaten egg, diluted with ¼ cup water to each egg, and then dip in dry bread crumbs. Fry in deep fat like oysters. Serve with catsup and cold slaw. Leftover creamed parsnips may be used by omitting the cream on this list of ingredients.

—*Cook Book: "New Process" Wick Oil Cook Stove*, circa 1910

Winter Succotash

This may be made with limas, horticulturals, garden beans, or white field beans. The latter are seldom used for succotash, but they make it very nicely. The method of proceeding in each case is the same. Boil the beans without soaking until three-fourths done. In the meantime put an equal amount (dry) of dried sweet corn with 3 quarts water and let it steep on the stove for 2 hours without boiling, then add to it the beans, and let them cook together gently until the beans are done. Serve warm and do not break the beans.

An excellent dish for breakfast is made from putting either beans or succotash into shallow dishes and covering with a little hot water. Heat slowly and do not stir while warming, as that makes them mussy. If they are likely to burn, put them back where there is not so much heat. Dish them up with a flat ladle so as to mash them as little as possible

—*Dr. Chase's Third Last and Complete Receipt Book and Household Physician*, 1903

Spinach with Eggs on Top

Cook spinach until tender in boiling salt water. Take up on a flat dish and lay over the top several poached or hard-boiled eggs; pour drawn butter and pepper over the top to serve.

EGGS & CHEESE

Hog's Head Cheese

Take a nicely cleaned hog's head, cover with water, and boil until very tender. Chop very finely and add salt, pepper, cloves, and allspice; pour the liquor it was boiled in over it and return to the fire; stir frequently until it thickens; skim off the fat that rises to the top. When very thick pour into molds; let it stand all night, then turn it out bottom upwards. If well done it will be a beautiful jelly.

—Mrs. J. R. Hutchison, Houston, Texas, *The First Texas Cookbook*, 1883

Dutch or Pot Cheese

Take thick sour milk and buttermilk, let it gradually heat (not boil), and when the whey is not milky pour all into a bag. Let it drain; do not squeeze it. When drained, mix thoroughly with the hands and season to taste. Some take all buttermilk, with a little sweet.

—*Healy & Bigelow's New Cook Book*, 1890

Fine Cottage Cheese

Let the milk be turned by rennet or by setting it in a warm place. It must not be heated, as the oily parts will then pass off, and the richness is lost. When fully turned, put in a coarse linen bag and hang it to drain several hours, until all the whey is out. Then mash it fine, salt it to taste, and thin it with good cream, or add but little cream, and roll it into balls. When thin, it is very fine with preserves or sugared fruit.

It also makes fine pudding, by thinning it with milk, adding eggs, sugar, and spice to taste, and baking it. Many persons use milk when turned to bonny-clabber for a dessert, putting on sugar and spice. Children are fond of it.

—*Miss Beecher's Housekeeper and Healthkeeper*, 1873

Shirred Eggs in Shredded Wheat Biscuit Baskets

Turn a cup of milk into a shallow dish. Prepare the biscuit baskets by crushing an oblong cavity in the top of six shredded-wheat biscuits with the bowl of a teaspoon and removing the inside shreds. Dip the bottom of the basket lightly in the milk and place in a buttered pan. Put little bits of butter in the bottom of biscuit baskets, salt and pepper lightly, and break an egg into each basket. Put little bits of butter on top, salt and pepper, and set in moderate oven until white of the egg is set. Remove from pan with pancake turner to warm plate and serve at once.

—*The Vital Question Cook Book*, 1908

Eggs in Disguise

Make a paste with 1 cup fine bread crumbs, a beaten egg, 2 tablespoons Underwood Deviled Ham, and a ½ cup of milk, or enough to moisten. Line buttered cups with this, and drop an egg from its shell into the center. Bake or steam until the eggs are firm—all the better if the yolk is hard. Loosen from the cup and turn each out on a small square of buttered toast. This quantity is sufficient for 4 to 6 eggs.

—*Taste the Taste and Some Cookery News*, circa 1910

English Monkey

1 bowl cheese
2 bowls bread crumbs
1 egg
sweet milk

Cut cheese in small pieces; add enough sweet milk to moisten the bread. Melt cheese in a frying pan, beat the egg, and mix with the bread crumbs; stir in the pan with the cheese until thoroughly mixed and cook a few moments. This is very like Welsh rarebit, but much better.

—*Healy & Bigelow's New Cook Book*, 1890

SALADS

Orange Salad

Cut up Sunkist Oranges, removing seeds and white fiber. Mix with a little sugar and serve with a cream dressing made as follows:

½ cup vinegar
½ teaspoon salt
½ cup sugar
1 dash cayenne
3 eggs
2 cups sweet or sour cream

Mix vinegar, salt, sugar, pepper, and yolks of eggs and put in double boiler, stirring constantly until creamy. Beat whites of eggs to stiff froth; when creamy, beat in whites while hot, then remove from fire. Put away to cool; when sufficiently cool, add cream, and it is ready to use.

—*Recipes for Dainty Dishes*, circa 1910s

Chestnut Salad

The chestnut salad is much in favor, and great is the variety both in method of preparation and serving. The chestnuts should in any case be cooked until very tender, cooled, and mixed with dressing.

Equal parts shredded celery and chestnuts is an appealing combination, or bananas, apples, celery, and chestnuts go well together. The fruit is pared, cored, and cut in slices and mixed with the chestnut meats. Dress with mayonnaise dressing and garnish with lettuce hearts.

—*The Way to a Man's Heart,* 1903

Salad à la Red Devil

Chop together lettuce, celery, and tomato for salad. Make a dressing with 1 egg, 1 tablespoon butter, ½ cup vinegar, salt, pepper, and mustard. Boil these, and when thickened by boiling, stir in 2 teaspoons Underwood Deviled Ham. Pour the mixture over the salad and serve on lettuce leaves.

—*Taste the Taste* and *Some Cookery News,* circa 1910

Italian Salad

    1 turnip
    1 carrot
    2 boiled potatoes
    1 beet-root
    1 onion

After cooking turnip and carrot in soup, slice them. When cold, mix with boiled potatoes and beet-root, also sliced. Add a very little onion and pour dressing on the mixture.

—*International Health Resort Recipes,* circa 1900

Let's Have a Little Joy Ride

...in the Underwood fairy-land, where everything is in "good taste" and everybody says "Taste the taste."

Here goes for the ride. Hold on tight or you may get spilled at the curves.

To the Waldorf went one of the newly rich; in search of good taste was he. Unable to understand the "manoo," he said unto the waiter, "Bring me $25 worth of ham and eggs." Ham was the best taste he knew—wise raw recruit of the newly rich.

And when you really think it over, is there any taste that actually does taste as good as ham? There is not.

And, in sooth, what could make a taster taste tastier than good boiled ham and 42 spices all ground up fine? That's what Underwood Deviled Ham is, and that's one reason why it tastes good.

However, all ham hasn't the said described taste. Some hams taste good and some taste punk.

But Underwood Ham has the taste—the home ham taste that you got from the farm-cured hams of your girlhood "on the old Brandywine."

—*Taste the Taste* and *Some Cookery News*, circa 1910
by W.M. Underwood Co.,
"*First Canners in America*,"
52 Fulton Street, Boston

Chicken Salad

2 cold boiled fowls
3 heads of celery
yolks of 9 hard-boiled eggs
½ pint sweet oil
½ pint vinegar

4 teaspoons mustard
1 teaspoon pepper
1 teaspoon salt

Finely chop the chicken and celery. Combine the remaining ingredients to prepare the dressing and mix with the chicken and celery. Let the salad stand about an hour before serving.

—Mrs. T. C. Armstrong, Galveston, Texas, *The First Texas Cookbook*, 1883

Summer Menu

And the offerings [of summer] arrive with such glorious progressiveness! First comes the strawberry, like a blush on the cheek of Mother Earth; then the berries and vegetables of more vigorous growth; then the stately, luscious melon, the charm and glory of the breakfast table; then corn, which is meat in nutrition; with the juicy apple, the pride of prince and peasant. Then we come to the pear and to the orchard—

> Where peaches grow with sunny dyes,
> Like maiden's cheeks when blushes rise,
> Where huge figs the branches bend.
> Where clusters from the vine distend.
> There is the feast which nature spreads.
> Let every man say grace in his heart and partake of it thankfully.

—*Dr. Chase's Third Last and Complete Receipt Book and Household Physician*, 1903

Cream Slaw

Put 1 pint vinegar, ½ cup sugar, and a walnut-sized piece of butter in a saucepan and let boil; stir 2 eggs, a pint of sour cream, and a teaspoon of flour, previously mixed, into the vinegar. Boil thoroughly and throw over a gallon of finely cut cabbage, previously sprinkled with a teaspoon each of salt, black pepper, and mustard.

—*Centennial Buckeye Cook Book*, 1876

Chow-Chow

peck of tomatoes
2 quarts green peppers
half a peck of onions
2 cabbages cut as for slaw
2 quarts mustard seed
gallon of vinegar
bit of alum
2 ounces cloves
2 ounces allspice

In a large firkin, put in a layer of sliced tomatoes, then one of onions, next one of peppers, lastly cabbage; sprinkle over with some of the mustard seed, repeat the layers again, and so on until you have used up the above quantity. Boil a gallon of vinegar, with a bit of alum, cloves, and allspice tied in a little bag; skim it well and turn into the firkin. Let it stand 24 hours, then pour the whole into a large kettle, and let it boil 5 minutes; turn into the firkin and keep for future use.

—*Sweet Home Cook Book*, 1888

Supper as the evening meal, has quietly accepted the neglected corner into which it has been thrust. . . . Except in the heat of summer, a hot dish should always be served for supper. . . . Soups are rarely served. Shellfish served raw or cooked in any form; small fish, broiled or fried; broiled steaks, chops, or chicken—all these are acceptable, especially when a hearty supper is required. But here, as with luncheon, made-over dishes are most often used. Potatoes, rice, hominy, and tomatoes in special forms, such as croquettes, scallops, etc., are served; other vegetables rarely, if ever. Eggs, salads, sandwiches in any form, hot breads, griddle cakes, and waffles—all these belong to supper. . . .

—*The Enterprising Housekeeper*, 1898

Chapter Thirteen

Recipes for Dinner: Soups and Meats

SOUPS

Vegetable Soup with Dumplings

Add 2 tablespoons of salt, a dash of cayenne, a small head of cabbage, a large onion, a stalk of celery, a stalk of leek chopped fine, and a strained can of tomatoes to a good-sized shank soup bone. Use, for drop dumplings, a ½ pint of flour, 2 eggs, a ½ teaspoon salt, and make them stiff enough to drop with a spoon into the soup.

—Mrs. Shaffner
P.O.E. Cook Book: Souvenir Edition, 1908

Chicken Gumbo No. 2

Fry one chicken, then fry a quart of thinly cut, salted, and floured okra in the hot lard where the chicken was fried. Take the chicken from the bones and mince it, then put it back into the frying pan with the okra. Add a quart of boiling water and let it cook five minutes. Now add a pint of sweet milk, 1 tablespoon of butter, salt, and pepper. Add a little flour and water smoothed together if it is not thick enough.

—Mrs. E.G. Myers
The Capitol Cook Book, 1899

Pea Soup

    1/4 pint peas
    1 small strip salt pork
    1 saltspoon salt
    celery seed
    1 small piece onion

Fry piece of onion until brown. Mix all, cover closely, and boil all together 4 or 5 hours. Rub through a colander.

—*The Cooking Garden*, 1885

Bisque Soup

Heat to almost boiling 1 quart of sweet milk in a porcelain vessel; add butter. Strain a can of tomatoes through a colander and roll three crackers to a powder. Add these to the milk with a pinch of soda. Let boil and remove from stove. Salt and pepper to taste.

—Mrs. L. B. Copes
The Capitol Cook Book, 1899

Calf's Head Soup

Let the butcher open the head wide. Take the brains from it and lay them into clean water with a little salt. Leave the tongue in the head when put on to boil with two gallons of water. When the tongue is tenderly boiled, take it out and let it get cold for making tongue salad. Boil the water down to half and strain it off clear for soup to one dozen guests. Take 2 quarts of this liquid and put it to boil. Brown 2 tablespoons of flour, then rub 1 tablespoon of butter into the brown flour until it comes to a cream, then add to the soup gradually, and stir well while adding. Season with salt and pepper and a little red pepper. While cooking, boil a small piece of thyme and half of an ordinary sized onion tied tight in a clean linen rag; this should be taken out of the soup when done. 1 tablespoon of mustard mixed with 1 tablespoon of wine and 1 glass of sherry wine should be put into the tureen before pouring in the hot soup.

Pick all skin from brains; beat 2 eggs lightly and add to the brains, then beat the eggs and brains together to a batter; add ½ a teacup of powdered cracker and 1 tablespoon flour to the brains and egg batter and beat together well. Then make this brain batter into cakes the size of a hickory nut and fry them brown in hot fat just before taking up soup. Send them to the table on a separate dish and serve them with the soup, two cakes to a plate of soup.

P.S.—Chop parsley very fine and boil it into the soup. You will find calf's head soup the most delicious soup in cookery. Study the recipe and remember it well.

—*What Mrs. Fisher Knows About Old Southern Cooking*, 1881

Mock Turtle Soup

Boil soup meat until tender and strain off the liquor. Chop a small onion and fry lightly. Gradually mix a teacup of browned flour into the liquor, put in the onion, a dozen allspice, ½ a dozen cloves, 4 little red peppers, and salt and pepper. Boil all together for half an hour. Have 2 or 3 hard-boiled eggs, chopped fine, in the tureen. When the soup is poured in the tureen, add 2 tablespoons wine or the juice of one lemon.

Mrs. T.W. House, *The Capitol Cook Book*, 1899

Dinner Menus

Macaroni Soup
Fricassee of Lamb   Riced Potatoes   Stewed Tomatoes
String Bean and Radish Salad   Fruit and Nuts

Cream of Celery Soup
Roast Beef   Franconia Potatoes   Yorkshire Pudding
Macaroni with Cheese   Tomato and Lettuce Salad
Chocolate Cream   Café Noir

Duchess Soup
Fried Fillets of Halibut   Shredded Potatoes   Hot Slaw
Beefsteak Pie
Irish Moss Blanc-Mange with Vanilla Wafers

—*The Boston Cooking-School Cook Book*, 1896

Spring Soup
Broiled Beefsteak   Royal Croquettes
Mashed Potatoes   Parsnips with Cream Sauce
Lettuce with Mayonnaise Dressing
Minnie's Lemon Pie   Nuts and Raisins

—*Ransom's Family Receipt Book*, 1885

DINNER MEATS

Lobster à la Newburg

Take the nicest part of 1 large lobster, cut in small slices, and put in chafing dish with a tablespoon of butter; season well with pepper and salt and pour 1 gill of wine over it. Cook for 10 minutes; add the beaten yolks of 3 eggs and a ½ pint of cream; let it come to a boil and serve immediately.

—*Sloan's Cook Book and Advice to Housekeepers*, 1905

Royal Croquettes

    3 small or 2 large sweetbreads
    1 boiled chicken
    1 heaping tablespoon flour
    1 pint cream
    6 eggs
    ½ cup butter
    1 tablespoon onion juice
    1 tablespoon chopped parsley
    1 teaspoon mace
    ½ lemon's worth of lemon juice
    cracker and bread crumbs
    salt and pepper

Let the sweetbreads stand in boiling water 5 minutes. Chop very fine, with the chicken, and add seasoning. Put 2 tablespoons butter in a stew pan with the flour. When it bubbles, gradually add the cream; then add the chopped mixture and stir until thoroughly heated. Take from the fire, add the lemon juice, and set away to cool. Salt and pepper the cracker and bread crumbs; roll croquettes into shape with the cracker crumbs. Dip in beaten eggs and then in cracker crumbs. Let stand until dry, then dip again in egg, and finally in bread crumbs—not too fine. Fry quickly in boiling fat.

—*Ransom's Family Receipt Book*, 1885

Fricassee of Veal

Dredge 1½ pounds veal steak cut from round with seasoned flour and fry in hot fat on bottom of pressure cooker until light brown. Add 1 onion, 2 stalks celery, and a sliced carrot. Cook for 15 minutes at 15 pounds pressure. Take meat up on platter and place vegetables around it. Add 1 cup boiling water and 2 tablespoons fat to the juice in which the meat has been cooked. Thicken with 2 tablespoons flour.

"Kook Kwick" Pressure Cooker Recipes, circa 1910s

Fricasseed Chicken

Chicken must be tender and cleaned well inside. Singe all pin feathers off over the fire. Boil 2 eggs hard, take the yolks and rub fine into 1 tablespoon butter, then add 1 tablespoon cornstarch dissolved into the least bit of water. Add all this together, well mixed and free from lumps. Have your chicken cut up before boiling, and stir the fricassee into the chicken just before sending to the table. Season with salt and pepper while cooking.

What Mrs. Fisher Knows About Old Southern Cooking, 1881

Beefsteak Pie

    2 pounds uncooked meat cut in 1-inch cubes
    1 onion chopped fine
    1 teaspoon salt

¼ teaspoon pepper
¼ pound suet freed of membrane and chopped fine
1 cup flour
1 tablespoon parsley chopped fine
1 cup Swift's beef extract or stock boiling hot

Put meat in deep pudding dish and sprinkle over it parsley, onion, salt, and pepper. To the suet add the flour, a pinch of salt, and sufficient ice water to moisten but not to make wet. Knead a little until it can be rolled out in a crust large enough to cover the top of the pudding dish. Pour the boiling stock over the meat. Spread the crust over the meat and cut a slit in the top. Brush over with milk and bake in a moderate oven. Serve in same dish with a napkin folded around it.

—*The Kitchen Encyclopedia*, 1911

Potatoes in Seven Ways for Dinner

❁ **SUNDAY**—*Mashed Potatoes.* Peel (thin), steam, place in a pan and mash, add milk, butter, and salt, and then beat like cake batter; the longer the better, till they are nice and light. This steaming and beating will be found a great improvement.

❁ **MONDAY**—*Baked Potatoes in their Jackets.* By the way, if any are left over, they may be warmed over by not peeling them till cold, and then slicing.

❁ **TUESDAY**—Peel and bake them with roast of beef.

❁ **WEDNESDAY**—*Potato Pudding.* Potatoes are sliced thin, as for frying, and allowed to remain in cold water ½ hour. Slices are then put in a pudding-dish, with salt, pepper, and mild milk—about ½ pint to an ordinary pudding dish. They are then put into an oven and baked for 1 hour. When taken out, a lump of butter the size of a hen's egg is cut into small bits and scattered over the top.

❁ **THURSDAY**—*Whole Steamed Potatoes.* Peel, steam, and serve whole.

❊ **Friday**—*Potatoes a la Pancake.* Peel, cut in thin slices lengthwise, sprinkle with pepper and salt, and fry in butter or beef drippings, turning like griddle cakes.

❊ **Saturday**—*Potatoes Boiled in their Jackets.*

—Dr. Chase's Third Last and Complete
Receipt Book and Household Physician, 1903

Spring Chicken Tirolienne

Joint the chicken, dust lightly with flour, and brown in plenty of butter, turning frequently so it will become brown on all sides. Add to it some boiled ham and diced fresh tomatoes, shallot, or onion chopped very fine. Simmer until tender. Garnish with fried apples and chopped parsley. Serve very hot.

—Ambassador Hotel, Chicago
Cuisine, 1912

Leg of Mutton Stuffed

Wash and wipe the mutton. Grate a pint of bread crumbs, season with salt and pepper, a teaspoon of sweet marjoram, 2 teaspoons of sage, and a ½ teaspoon of sweet basil (all dried and rubbed fine). Chop a medium-sized onion and put it over the fire in a small saucepan with butter the size of a large egg, stew for 5 minutes, pour over the bread crumbs, and stir in thoroughly. Make a deep incision on the long side of the leg parallel with the bone and push the dressing in, all through the length of the leg. Skewer it at the opening where it was stuffed and season the leg with pepper and salt. Dust it with flour and roast it 2 hours in a hot oven, keeping a little water in the pan to baste it with, which should be done every 15 or 20 minutes. Thicken the gravy with browned flour and put spoonfuls over the meat when you place it on the dish; serve the remainder in a gravy boat. To be eaten with a currant jelly.

—*Sweet Home Cook Book*, 1888

Chapter Fourteen

Recipes for Desserts and Beverages

DESSERTS

Pineapple Bavarian Cream

Soak ½ package of gelatin two hours in ½ cup cold water. Chop a pint of pineapple fine and put it on with a small teacup of sugar. Simmer 20 minutes. Add the gelatin, and strain immediately into a tin basin. Rub as much of the pineapple as possible through the sieve. Beat until it begins to thicken, and add a pint of cream, which has been whipped to a froth. When well mixed, pour into the mold, and put away to harden. Serve with whipped cream.

—Dr. Earl S. Sloan, Boston
Sloan's Cook Book and Advice to Housekeepers, 1905

Peanut Drops

>2 tablespoons butter
>¼ cup sugar
>1 egg
>1 teaspoon baking powder
>¼ teaspoon salt
>½ cup flour
>2 tablespoons milk
>½ cup finely chopped peanuts

Cream the butter, add sugar, and egg well beaten. Mix and sift baking powder, salt, and flour; add to first mixture; then add milk and peanuts. Drop from a teaspoon on a slightly buttered sheet 1 inch apart, and place 1 half-peanut on top of each. Bake 12 to 15 minutes in a slow oven. This recipe will make 24 little cakes.

—*Catering for Special Occasions,* 1911

Cottage Pudding

Bake in a greased pudding dish 3 tablespoons melted butter, 1 cup sugar, 2 cups flour, 2 beaten eggs, 2 teaspoons baking powder, and 1 cup sweet milk. Serve with a rich sauce.

☛ Pudding Sauces ☚

✺ **HARD SAUCE NO. 2.** Cream 1 cup butter and 2 cups sugar, and flavor to taste.

✺ **GOOD SAUCE.** Beat 1 cup sugar and ½ cup butter to a cream; add 1 egg beaten well, ½ cup wine, and 3 tablespoons water. Stir well and set it over a boiling teakettle a few minutes before serving.

✺ **VERY NICE SAUCE.** Beat the yolk of 1 egg with ½ cup white sugar and a tablespoon of cornstarch; stir in 3 tablespoons boiling water; set it over a teakettle to keep warm. Just as you take it to the table, stir in lightly the white of egg beaten with other ½ cup of sugar, a little nutmeg, and a spoonful of brandy or wine.

🏵 **Confederate sauce for cake.** 2 cups sugar, 1 tablespoon butter, yolk of 1 egg beaten well. Mix well and pour in ¼ pint of boiling milk; add a glass of wine and season with nutmeg.

—*The Capitol Cook Book*, 1899

Charlotte Russe

1 pint sweet cream
4 eggs
3 tablespoons sugar

Beat first the whites of the eggs to a light froth; then beat the cream to a light froth; next beat the sugar into the eggs; then beat 2 additional tablespoons of sugar in the cream lightly; then add the cream and eggs together. Flavor with 1½ teaspoons of best vanilla and stir well. Lay your cakes, lady fingers, in the mold, well at the bottom and close together around the sides. Pour the russe on the cake and set it in the icebox. See that the mold is in perfect order. Serve on table with teaspoons on small saucers. Use granulated sugar in all sweets.

—*What Mrs. Fisher Knows About Old Southern Cooking*, 1881

Apple Fritters

Beat 3 eggs lightly and stir in 1 teaspoon salt, 1 teaspoon sugar, and the grated rind of half a lemon and its juice. Also add 1 pint milk, 2 cups chopped apple, and 2 cups flour. Stir it all together well and fry in large skillet or bake them on a griddle as pancakes. Sift sugar over them and send to the table.

—*Sweet Home Cook Book*, 1888

Hermits

    2 cups brown sugar
    2 eggs well beaten
    ¾ cup butter and lard mixed
    1 tablespoon cinnamon
    1 teaspoon cloves
    6 tablespoons sour milk
    1 teaspoon soda dissolved in milk
    1 cup chopped raisins
    1 cup chopped walnuts
    flour

Mix all ingredients and add flour to make it stiff enough to drop from a spoon. Bake in buttered tins.

—*Cupid at Home in the Kitchen,* circa 1910

Chocolate Tarts

Rub ½ cake of grated baker's chocolate smooth in 3 tablespoons milk and heat to boiling over the fire, then stir in 1 tablespoon cornstarch dissolved in water. Stir 5 minutes until well thickened; remove from the fire and pour into a bowl. Beat the yolks of 4 eggs and the whites of 2 eggs with 4 tablespoons sugar; when the chocolate mixture is almost cold, put all together with 2 teaspoons vanilla, 1 saltspoon salt, ½ teaspoon cinnamon, and stir until light. Bake in open shells of pastry. When done, cover with a meringue made of the whites of 2 eggs and 2 tablespoons sugar flavored with 1 teaspoon lemon juice. Eat cold. These are nice for tea, baked in patty pans.

—*Common Sense in the Household,* 1871

Lady Fingers

    3 eggs
    ⅓ cup powdered sugar

⅓ cup flour
⅛ teaspoon salt
¼ teaspoon vanilla

Beat whites of 3 eggs until stiff and dry, add sugar gradually, and continue beating. Then add yolks of 2 eggs, beaten until thick and lemon-colored, and flavoring. Cut and fold in flour mixed and sifted with salt. Shape 4½ inches long and 1 inch wide on a tin sheet covered with unbuttered paper, using a pastry bag and tube. Sprinkle with powdered sugar and bake 8 minutes in a moderate oven. Remove from paper with a knife.

—*Catering for Special Occasions*, 1911

Ginger Snaps

1 cup molasses
2 tablespoons butter
1 tablespoon ginger
1 teaspoon saleratus
flour

Boil the molasses and stir in the butter, ginger, and saleratus, rolled fine; stir the flour in while hot; roll out thin, cut, and bake.

—*Dr. Chase's Third Last and Complete Receipt Book and Household Physician*, 1903

Peach Tapioca Pudding

Soak a ½ pint of tapioca in cold water for 2 or 3 hours, then set it on the stove until it boils. Sweeten with white sugar; peel and slice ripe peaches to nearly fill a baking dish; sprinkle over them white sugar, then pour over the tapioca, and bake slowly for 1 hour. Eat with cream and sugar.

—*Sweet Home Cook Book*, 1888

Delicious Desserts for Summer and Autumn Dinners

Summer

SUNDAY
Fruit Cream
Angel's Food
Roman Punch
Almond Drops

MONDAY
Cherry Pie

TUESDAY
Peach Cottage Pudding
Hard Sauce

WEDNESDAY
Strawberry Shortcake

THURSDAY
Strawberry Sherbet
White Pound Cake

FRIDAY
Charlotte Russe
Ring Jumbles

SATURDAY
Peach Pie

Autumn

SUNDAY
Peach Ice Cream
Caramel Cake

MONDAY
Railroad Pudding
Foaming Sauce

TUESDAY
Custard Pie

WEDNESDAY
Velvet Blanc Mange
Sugar Cookies

THURSDAY
Pumpkin Pie

FRIDAY
Coconut Pie

SATURDAY
Apple Fritters
White Wine Sauce

—*Dr. Price's Delicious Desserts*, 1904

Apple Lemon Pudding

    6 spoons grated or cooked and strained apple
    3 lemons—pulp, rind, and juice, all grated
    ½ pound melted butter
    sugar to the taste
    7 eggs well beaten

Mix all and bake with or without paste. It can be made still plainer by using 9 spoons of apple, 1 lemon, ⅔ cup butter, and 3 eggs.

—*Miss Beecher's Housekeeper and Healthkeeper*, 1873

Plum Pudding to Englishmen's Taste, in Rhyme

To make plum-pudding to Englishmen's taste,
So all may be eaten and nothing to waste,
Take of raisins, and currants, and bread-crumbs, all round;
Also suet from oxen, and flour a pound,
Of citron well candied, or lemon as good,
With molasses and sugar, eight ounces, I would,
Into this first compound, next must be hasted
A nutmeg well grated, ground ginger well tasted,
With salt to preserve it, of such a teaspoonful;
Then of milk half a pint, and of fresh eggs take six;
Be sure after this that you properly mix.
Next tie up in a bag, just as round as you can,
Put into a capacious and suitable pan,
Then boil for eight hours just as hard as you can.

—*Dr. Chase's Third Last and Complete Receipt Book and Household Physician*, 1903

Vanilla Ice Cream

The foundation given in this rule is suitable for all kinds of ice cream. Let a generous pint of milk come to a boil. Beat 1 cup of sugar, ½ scant cup of flour, and 2 eggs together, and stir into the boiling milk. Cook 20 minutes, stirring often. Set away to cool, and when cool add another cup sugar, 1 tablespoon vanilla extract, and 1 quart cream, and freeze.

—*Sloan's Cook Book and Advice to Housekeepers*, 1905

Dr. Price's Ice Cream Sugar

By the use of Dr. Price's Delicious Ice Cream Sugar, every housewife can, at a moment's notice, place before her family an Ice Cream remarkable for smoothness, palatableness, and purity. It is always ready for immediate use—no flavoring, color or cooking necessary. Simply add the contents of one package to one pint of milk and one pint of cream, dissolve, and freeze. Ice Cream Sugar is without a parallel in the facility and quickness with which it is made into a delicate, delicious desert. It is one of the very latest additions to the many superior articles produced by Dr. Price, the housewife's friend and pure food expert.

LIST OF FLAVORS:
VANILLA, LEMON, ORANGE, MAPLE, STRAWBERRY, PISTACHIO, PEACH

—*Dr. Price's Delicious Deserts*, 1904

BEVERAGES

Cocoa

To 1 pint milk and 1 pint cold water add 3 tablespoons grated cocoa. Boil 15 or 20 minutes, milling or whipping. Sweeten to taste, at the table. Some persons like a piece of orange peel boiled with it.

—*Housekeeping in Old Virginia*, 1879

How to Make Good Coffee

Mix 1 egg thoroughly with 2 heaping teaspoons coffee, put into the coffeepot, and pour on it 2 cups freshly boiling water. Boil 5 minutes, stir well with a fork, and set on the back of the stove to keep hot for 5 minutes. Add ½ cup water, pour out a little coffee, and pour it back again to clean the grounds from the spout, then let stand 10 minutes and be careful not to shake the pot when serving. Serve with the best and richest cream. However, in the absence of this luxury, a good substitute may be found in boiled milk prepared as follows: place fresh new milk in a pan or pail, set where it will slowly simmer but not boil or reach the boiling pint; stir frequently to keep the cream from separating and rising to the top; let simmer until it is rich, thick, and creamy.

—*Cereal Foods and How to Cook Them*, 1899

Whipped Syllabub

Take a lump of sugar and rub it on the outside of a lemon until colored, then put it into a pint of cream and sweeten to taste. Squeeze in the juice of a lemon, add a glass of sherry or Madeira, mill to a froth, and take off the froth as it rises. Drain well in a sieve, then half fill a glass with red wine, and pile up froth as high as possible.

Loving Cup

1 bottle Scotch ale
1 pint sherry
¼ pound sugar
1 bottle soda water
1 small piece toasted bread
grated nutmeg
4 slices lemon

In the first place, the sugar must be melted and strained; then place it in a cup holding 3 quarts water, then add the wine and the ale; stir these up well. Just before serving, add the soda water; and on the froth, a little grated nutmeg. Place in the toast and lemon, and take it to the table; it should be drunk immediately. This is considered by many persons to be the best cup that was ever made.

—*Peterson's Magazine*, March 1868

The French coffee is reputed the best in the world, and a thousand voices have asked, What is it about the French coffee? In the first place, then, the French coffee is coffee, and not chicory, or rye, or beans, or peas. In the second place, it is freshly roasted, whenever made—roasted with great care and evenness in a little revolving cylinder which makes part of the furniture of every kitchen, and which keeps in the aroma of the berry. It is never overdone, so as to destroy the coffee flavor, which is in nine cases out of ten the fault of the coffee we meet with. Then it is ground, and placed in a coffeepot with a filter, through which it percolates in clear drops, the coffeepot standing on a heated stove to maintain the temperature. The nose of the coffeepot is stopped up to prevent the escape of the aroma during this process. The extract thus obtained is a perfectly clear, dark fluid, known as café noir, or black coffee. It is black only because of its strength, being in fact almost the very essential oil of coffee.

—Harriet Beecher Stowe,
House and Home Papers, 1869

Floating Island

Beat the yolks of 6 eggs with the juice of 4 lemons, sweeten it to your taste, and stir it into a quart of boiling milk until it thickens, then pour it into a dish. Whip the whites of the eggs to a stiff froth and put it on the top of the cream.

Miss Beecher's Housekeeper and Healthkeeper, 1873

The Sighs of Love

Mix 1 gallon proof spirit, 1 gallon water, 7 pounds sugar, and 45 drops attar of roses; use cochineal to produce a pale pink color.

Buttermilk

Farmers' families seldom appreciate what a delicious and healthful drink they have in homemade buttermilk. It was the fashionable drink in New York last summer, and brokers, bankers, and merchants indulged in it at three cents a glass, from street stands or wagons. Ice is not an essential where a beverage can be stood to cool in a porous earthen jar in a cold cellar or milk room, such as belongs to every farmhouse.

—*Healy & Bigelow's New Cook Book*, 1890

A Bishop

Stick cloves in the rind of a lemon or orange and roast it a long time before a slow fire. Put equal quantities of cinnamon, cloves, allspice, and mace into a little water, and boil them until the whole strength is extracted. Boil a bottle of Port or claret wine and put the roast lemon and spice into it. Sweeten, add the juice of half a lemon, and grate in some nutmeg. Serve hot with lemon and spice floating in it.

Hot Coffee and Soda

For temperance advocates, hot black coffee mixed with soda water is a good substitute for the spirituous winter drinks. Make black coffee as follows: ¼ pound of good coffee and ¼ ounce of ground chicory infused in a quart of boiling water—but not actually boiled—will make medium strong coffee. Boiling coffee makes it very black and bitter. Use hot black coffee and soda water in equal proportions, with a palatable addition of cream syrup or condensed milk and sugar.

—*Miss Corson's Practical American Cookery and Household Management*, 1885

CHAPTER FIFTEEN

*C*OMPANY EXPECTED: RECIPES FOR SPECIAL GATHERINGS

TEAS & LUNCHEONS

For an afternoon out-of-door tea ... a pretty way to serve sandwiches is to roll them and tie them with different colored ribbons; a stoned olive can be put inside each one. Strawberries and cream, fancy cakes, Newport whips, iced tea, and seltzer lemonade will be sufficient for refreshments.

*F*ive O'Clock Tea

Put 3 teaspoons tea in teapot and pour on 2 cups boiling water. Let stand 3 minutes and strain into teacups. Serve with cut sugar and cream.

—*Catering for Special Occasions*, 1911

Russian Tea

Make same as Five O'Clock Tea and allow ½ teaspoon lemon juice and a thin slice of lemon from which seeds have been removed to each cup. Sweeten with cut sugar to suit individual taste. Many prefer the addition of 3 whole cloves or a candied cherry.

—*Catering for Special Occasions*, 1911

Austrian Coffee for Teas and Receptions

A coffee of the above name, sometimes served at teas and receptions, is a cold, strong coffee, creamed and sweetened. It is served in small glasses, with a tablespoon of ice cream added in each glass after the coffee is put in.

—*Mrs. Seely's Cook Book*, 1902

Gold or Silver Cake

Mix 2 cups flour, ½ cup milk, ½ cup butter, 1 cup sugar, yolks of 3 eggs, 1 teaspoon soda, and 2 teaspoons cream of tartar. May be made the same as gold cake, only use a little more butter.

—*Sweet Home Cook Book*, 1888

As we look to France for the best coffee, so we must look to England for the perfection of tea. The tea kettle is as much an English institution as aristocracy or the Prayer-Book; and when one wants to know exactly how tea should be made, one has only to ask how a fine old English housekeeper makes it. The first article of her faith is that the water must not merely be hot, not merely have boiled a few moments since, but be actually boiling at the moment it touches the tea. Hence, though servants in England are vastly better trained than with us, this delicate mystery is seldom left to their hands. Tea-making belongs to the drawing room, and high-born ladies preside at "the bubbling and loud-hissing urn," and see that all due rites and solemnities are properly performed—that the cups are hot, and that the infused tea waits the exact time before the libations commence.

—Harriet Beecher Stowe,
House and Home Papers, 1869

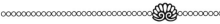

Delicious Desserts for Spring Teas or Luncheons

SUNDAY   Lemon Jelly ❦ Gold Cake

MONDAY   Floating Island ❦ Chocolate Cake

TUESDAY   Sliced Oranges ❦ Philadelphia Jumbles

WEDNESDAY   Boston Cream Cakes

THURSDAY   Currant and Raspberry Tarts with whipped cream

FRIDAY   Cup Custard ❦ Fruit Cookies

SATURDAY   Baked Sweet Apples with whipped cream

Clove Cake

—*Dr. Price's Delicious Desserts*, 1904

Scalloped Cheese, Nice for Tea

Take three slices of bread well buttered, first cutting off the brown crust. Grate a quarter of a pound of any good cheese. Lay the bread in a baking dish and sprinkle over it the grated cheese; salt and pepper to taste. Mix 4 well-beaten eggs with 3 cups milk and pour this over the bread and cheese. Bake in a hot oven until brown. This is nice for tea.

—*The Capitol Cook Book*, 1899

Jam Jumbles

½ cup butter
1 cup sugar
1 egg
½ teaspoon soda
½ cup sour milk

¼ teaspoon salt
flour
raspberry jam

Cream the butter; add sugar gradually, well-beaten egg, soda mixed with milk, salt, and flour to make a soft dough. Chill, roll to ¼ inch in thickness, and shape, using a round cutter. On the centers of half the pieces put raspberry jam. Make three small openings in remaining halves (forming a triangle), using a thimble, and put pieces together. Press edges slightly, and bake in a rather hot oven, so jumbles may keep in good shape.

—*Catering for Special Occasions*, 1911

> *In* a moment thirty people were round the well-lighted table, and in another were served with the edibles—biscuit, tongue, marmalade, delicious cake, fruited and plain, tarts, dishes of froth and amber, preserved fruits and cream; in short, all that the limits of Thornbury, distant from the city, allowed.
>
> —"The Tea-Party," 1871

Green Gooseberry Tart

Top and tail the gooseberries. Put into a porcelain kettle with enough water to prevent burning, and stew slowly until they break. Take them off, sweeten well, and set aside to cool. When cold, pour into pastry shells, and bake with a top crust of puff-paste. Brush with beaten egg while hot; set back in the oven to glaze for 3 minutes. Eat cold.

—*Common Sense in the Household*, 1871

What Will You Have?

Thank you—a plate of any thing. Have you been to a country tea-party before?

No, never; I like it. Why do so many keep utter silence, though? A good many have only opened their mouths to eat, not to speak.

It is our way. Tomorrow they will speak fast enough; we shall be turned into hash.

Yet you invite such?

Oh, we must invite each other; we live so. Our events often come from these insignificant meetings.

Does that elderly young lady enjoy herself, for instance? And he pointed to a silent spinster who held her third teacup, and who was looking everywhere with wide eyes.

Certainly. She has the pattern of all our dresses in her head, and can set forth our manners, and repeat all that has been said, at any moment from this table.

The bashful young man, who laughs so much, is he really entertained?

He is bashful here; but tomorrow, in the shops or loafing-places, he will be very bold and sneering in his remarks upon my attempt at society.

I see, a tea-party is like others; or human nature in general.

—"The Tea-Party," 1871

Sandwich Fillings for Picnics and Daytime Gatherings

- *Vegetable*: 1 ounce rhubarb juice, 1 ounce peanuts, 1 ounce carrots, and 1 ounce celery.
- Cottage cheese and chopped dates.
- Grated cheese and minced onion.
- Lettuce, cream cheese, and chopped olives.
- Equal parts dates, peanut butter, and cream cheese.
- Crisp cucumber, dry and dip in dressing and place between binders.
- Peel and grate 1 tart apple; mix ½ cup cream cheese and 1 tablespoon cream. Add apple and mix.

- ☞ Flaked peanuts moistened with lemon juice and honey.
- ☞ Lettuce and peanut butter mixed with lemon juice. Put peanut butter mixture on buttered bread and lay on lettuce leaves.

—International Health Resort Recipes, ca. 1900

Watercress Sandwiches

Wash well some watercress, and then dry them in a cloth, pressing out every atom of moisture; then mix with the cresses finely chopped hard-boiled eggs seasoned with salt and pepper. Have a stale loaf and some fresh butter; with a sharp knife, cut as many thin slices as will be required for 2 dozen sandwiches; then cut the cress into small pieces, removing the stems, and place it between each slice of bread and butter, with a slight sprinkling of lemon juice; press down the slices hard and cut them sharply on a board into small squares, leaving no crust.

—The White House Cook Book, 1887

Honor Sandwiches for St. Valentine's Tea

Cut white bread in ¼-inch slices and shape with heart cutter. Spread with pimento butter, put together in pairs, and arrange on a fancy plate covered with a doily.

Pimento butter—Cream 2 tablespoons butter, add 1 canned pimento forced through a sieve, and work until thoroughly blended; then season with salt.

—Catering for Special Occasions, 1911

Afternoon Teas

A new wrinkle at afternoon teas is the service of crackers or wafers spread with Sunkist Orange. Put together sandwich fashion and heat in the oven just long enough to allow the flavor and juice of the fruit to penetrate the cracker and soften it slightly.

—Recipes for Dainty Dishes,
circa 1910s

RECIPES FOR OTHER OCCASIONS

Fourth of July Punch

1 cup sugar
½ cup water
1 can sliced pineapple, cut in pieces
2 lemons
2 oranges
½ cup raspberry syrup
¼ cup brandy
1 pint bottle Moselle wine
1 pint bottle Apollinaris

Boil sugar and water 5 minutes; add juice from lemons and oranges as well as remaining ingredients. Pour over a cake of ice.

—*Catering for Special Occasions*, 1911

Thanksgiving Mince Pie

2 pounds lean fresh beef, boiled, and when cold, chopped fine
1 pound beef suet, cleared of strings and minced to powder
5 pounds apples, pared and chopped
2 pounds raisins, seeded and chopped
1 pound Sultana raisins, washed and picked over
2 pounds currants, washed and carefully picked over

¾ pound citron, cut up fine
2 tablespoons cinnamon
1 tablespoon powdered nutmeg
2 tablespoons mace
1 tablespoon cloves
1 tablespoon allspice
1 tablespoon fine salt
2¼ pounds brown sugar
1 quart brown sherry
1 pint best brandy

Mincemeat made by this recipe will keep all winter in a cool place. Keep in stone jars, tied over with double covers. Add a little more liquor (if it should dry out), when you make up a batch of pies. Let the mixture stand at least 24 hours after it is made before it is used. When ready to make pies, lay strips of pastry, notched with a jagging-iron, in a cross-bar pattern, upon the pie, instead of a top-crust.

—*Common Sense in the Household*, 1871

Pumpkin Pie

Stew a kettle-full of pumpkin and press it through a colander. For a quart of the stewed pumpkin, use about 1 pint or a little more of sweet milk, 2 cups sugar, 3 eggs, and 1 teaspoon ginger; bake in a crust in a deep pie plate.

—*Dr. Chase's Third Last and Complete Receipt Book and Household Physician*, 1903

Thanksgiving Dinner

For the table I prefer a white cloth with fancy border and napkins to match. A dash of color livens up the table in the bleak November when flowers cannot be had in profusion. Casters in the center, of course, flanked by tall celery glasses. At each end, glass fruit dishes filled with apples and nuts. A bottle of pepper sauce near the casters, a mold of jelly by the platter of turkey, and small side dishes of chopped cabbage garnished with rings of cold boiled eggs. The purple cabbage makes the handsomest-looking dishes. Serve the soup from tureens into soup dishes, handing around to the guests. After this comes the piece de resistance, "Thanksgiving turkey." A piece of dark meat with a spoonful of gravy, and one of white with a bit of jelly and a baked potato (I should prefer a spoonful of mashed) should be served on each plate, leaving the other vegetables to be passed afterward with the roast pig. After this the salad, and then the plates should be taken away and the dessert served. Then come the apples and nuts, the tea and coffee, well seasoned with grandpa's old-time stories, grandma's quaint sayings, and kind words and merry repartees from all.

—Dr. Chase's Third Last and Complete
Receipt Book and Household Physician, 1903

Roast Goose

Stuff the goose with potato dressing. Truss and dredge well with salt, pepper, and flour. Roast (if 8 pounds) 1¼ hour. No butter is required for goose, since it is so fat. Serve with applesauce.

Potato Dressing:

- 6 potatoes
- 1 tablespoon salt
- 1 tablespoon pepper
- 1 teaspoon sage
- 2 tablespoons onion juice
- 2 tablespoons butter

Boil potatoes; pare them, then mash them fine and light. Combine all.

—*Sloan's Cook Book and Advice to Housekeepers*, 1905

Menu for Christmas Dinner

Consommé   Bread Sticks

Olives   Celery   Salted Pecans

Roast Goose   Potato Stuffing   Apple Sauce

Duchess Potatoes   Cream of Lima Beans

Chicken Croquettes with Green Peas

Dressed Lettuce with Cheese Straws

English Plum Pudding   Brandy Sauce

Frozen Pudding   Assorted Cake   Bonbons

Crackers   Cheese   Café Noir

—*The Boston Cooking-School Cook Book*, 1896

Wedding Cake

50 eggs
5 pounds sugar
5 pounds flour
5 pounds butter
15 pounds raisins
3 pounds citron
10 pounds currants
1 pint brandy
¼ ounce cloves
1 ounce cinnamon
4 ounces mace
4 ounces nutmeg

This makes 43½ pounds and keeps 20 years.

—*Centennial Buckeye Cookbook*, 1876

Chapter Sixteen

For the Lady as Hostess

Receiving Your Husband's Guests

Especially, let your welcome be ready and hearty when your husband brings home an unexpected guest.

UNDERSTAND HIM. Take care he understands clearly that this is his prerogative and that the rules by which you would govern the visits of your own sex are not applicable to his. Men rarely set seasons for their visits. They snatch an hour or two with an old chum or new friend out of the hurry of business life, as one stoops to pluck a stray violet from a dusty roadside. Your husband must take his chances when he can get them.

WELCOME HIS GUESTS GLADLY. If he can walk home, arm in arm, with the school fellow he has not seen in ten years, not only fearlessly, but gladly anticipatory of your pleasure at the sight of him; if, when the stranger is presented to you, you receive him as your friend because he is your husband's and seat him to a family dinner, plain, but nicely served, and eaten in cheerfulness of heart; if the children are well behaved and your attire that of a lady who has not lost the desire to look her best in her husband's eyes, then you have added to the links of steel that knit your husband's heart to yours.

My wife, I will not deny, was a little elated at the idea of having a city Editor to dinner; but when I repeated, one by one, your extraordinary expectations, she became very thoughtful and silent. Why you see, sir, the "spring chickens" we could count upon, by-and-bye; but the "trout," the "woodcock," the "snipe," the "wild ducks," and, coolest of propositions, that all these should be brought on consecutively, keeping half a dozen cooks busy, and quite confounding my father and my dear old aunt with such unheard-of proceedings—all these, and ices and wines, in our quiet country home—Oh, sir, I blush at the thought of it. Moreover, I withdraw the invitation. Don't come to dinner. I forbid it.

—Country Margins and Rambles of a Journalist, 1855

Guests in Your Home

REQUEST NOTIFICATION OF A VISIT. Do not be ashamed to say to your nearest of kin or the confidante of your school days, "Always let me know when to look for you." If you are the woman I take you to be—methodical, industrious, and ruling your household according to just and firm laws of order and punctuality—you need this notice.

UPON INVITATION, STATE THE LENGTH OF THE VISIT. Mention the day when you would be happy to receive them and the length of time of their visit. Perhaps a young lady is invited to make a visit in the country, or in the city, and no mention is made of days, weeks, or months, for its limit; therefore, she is utterly at a loss to know what amount of clothing, etc., she may require.

WELCOME THEM SIMPLY. Welcome the coming guest with a few, simple, pleasant, easy words and without ostentatious cordiality; without gushing declarations of friendship; without paralyzing his arm by an interminable shaking of hands; without hurry, flourish, and due anxiety to have his trunk carried up to his room; or sandwiching between every sentence an anxious appeal to make himself entirely at home—an appeal which usually operates to make one feel as much away from home as possible.

ENABLE HIM TO HELP HIMSELF. The art of hospitality consists in making the guest forget that he is a guest and in leaving to him the exercise of his senses and of responsibility, at least so far that, finding what he needs at his hand, he may help himself.

HAVE THE FIRE READY. It is merciless to invite friends to visit you in cold weather without providing a fire in their bedroom or dressing room. Neither is it courteous to wait until they arrive, and then inquire, "Would you like a fire?" Therefore, if you cannot afford to make your friends comfortable, do not invite them; at least in the wintry season.

A HOME PREPARED FOR A GUEST LOOKS THUS:
- The additional place is set at the table.
- Your spare bed, which yesterday was tossed into a heap, has both mattresses aired, is covered lightly with a thin spread, and is made up with fresh sheets that have not gathered damp.
- The room is bright and dustless.
- Towels are aplenty, fresh soap is in the dish, fresh ink in the inkstand, fresh pen in the holder, stationery at hand, and the pin cushion well supplied with pins.
- Candles, matches, and water are on the stand by the bedside.
- The drawers of closet and bureau are empty and, if sachets are not supplied, smooth white paper is spread in them.
- The dainty dish is prepared for dinner or tea so as to be off your mind.

- Your husband knows whom he is to see at his homecoming.
- The children are clean and on the qui vive—children's instincts are always hospitable.
- The guest's welcome is given in the air of such a house. Perhaps, as she lays aside her traveling dress, she smiles at your "ceremonious, old-maidish ways" and marvels that so good a manager should deem such forms necessary with an old friend.

Receive unannounced visitors happily. Since unlooked-for visitors will occasionally drop in upon the best-regulated families, make it your study to receive them gracefully and cordially. If they care enough for you to turn aside from their regular route to tarry a day, night, or week with you, it would be churlish not to show appreciation of the favor in which you are held. Make them welcome to the best you can offer at so short notice, and let no preoccupied air or troubled smile be token to your perturbation.

Put up luncheon upon their departure. It is a graceful act to provide a pasteboard box of lunch for a departing visitor, as during a long journey the opportunities for a comfortable meal are often lacking. Most ladies, myself among the number, would usually prefer to go without a dinner than to hurry to the counter of a railway dining saloon, give an order, and attempt to eat and drink with one eye on the clock and the other on the cars.

Chicken Lunch for Traveling

Cut a young chicken down the back; wash and wipe dry; season with salt and pepper; put in a dripping pan and bake in a moderate oven three-quarters of an hour. This is much better for traveling lunch than when seasoned with butter.

—*The White House Cook Book*, 1887

Chapter Seventeen

For the Lady Visitor, the Lady Caller, and the Lady Correspondent

The Visitor

There is the art, too, of making oneself agreeable as a guest.

Notify your hostess in advance. Laying to your conduct the line and plummet of the Golden Rule, never pay a visit (I use the word in contra-distinction to "call") without notifying your hostess-elect of your intention thus to favor her. Perhaps once in ten thousand times, your friend—be she mother, sister, or intimate acquaintance—may be enraptured at your unexpected appearance, traveling satchel in hand, at her door to pass a day, a night, or a month. But the chances are so greatly in favor of the probability that you will upset her household arrangements, abrade her temper, or put her to undue trouble or embarrassment, that it is hardly worth your while to risk so much in order to gain so little.

Adapt yourself. Endeavor to conform, without apparent effort, to the arrangements of the family with whom you board and to the manners and customs of the people around you, as far as they do not compromise your principles of good morals and good taste. If you don't like a thing, let it alone; eat nothing, and by the next meal you may be glad to eat anything.

Journey by Stage Coach from Marshall to Austin

In the autumn [of 1858] my father was elected the State Senate and we made preparations for our journey to Austin. There were no railroads across the State in those days, and the hundreds of miles had to be traversed by private conveyance, or by stage coach.

We decided to make the expedition in our old-fashioned family carriage, drawn by a pair of stout horses. . . . My brother came with us on horseback. We made the journey in easy stages—our luggage, of course, being sent on by coach. We would drive about thirty miles a day—never more; stopping in the middle of the day for an hour or so, when the horses would be thoroughly rested and fed, and we would have our luncheon. At night, we always stopped at a convenient farmhouse, the location of which had been previously learned, and whose owners were accustomed, in a country where there were no inns, to receive occasional travelers.

. . . I recall very vividly the evening when we came in sight of the city of Austin: the brilliant autumn sunset, the invigorating air, the lovely view of the surrounding country, the sound of the horses' feet ringing on the hard, smooth road, as we rolled along, down the slope that brought us to our journey's end—half way across the State of Texas, in ten days.

—*A Southern Girl in '61—The War-Time Memories of a Confederate Senator's Daughter*, 1905

Take congeniality. Be cheerful, be kind, be considerate, be accommodating. Shun argument and controversy on any and all subjects. Do not obtrude your political or religious sentiments. Let your courtesy come out naturally, and if religious, don't be a Pharisee.

Avoid dining rudeness. Blowing soup or pouring tea and coffee into the saucer to cool is evidence of a lack of knowledge of the usage of good society. Beware, lest you make that disagreeable sound in eating soup which is not only offensive to the ear but is a positive rudeness. Do not eat all on your plate and do not clean it up with your bread. In a dinner of several courses, it is unusual for a guest to ask for any dish a second time.

Reciprocate your host's welcome. A dinner invitation should always be returned during the social season; that is, before people separate for the summer. If the recipient has not an establishment which admits of giving a dinner in return, a ride or drive in the country, a good restaurant dinner, or a theatre party in the city is considered a social equivalent.

Hints for Plains Travelers

- The best seat inside a stagecoach is the one next to the driver... you will get less than half the bumps and jars than on any other seat. When any old "sly Eph," who traveled thousands of miles on coaches, offers through sympathy to exchange his back or middle seat with you, don't do it.

- Never ride in cold weather with tight boots or shoes, nor close-fitting gloves. Bathe your feet before starting in cold water, and wear loose overshoes and gloves two or three sizes too large.

- When the driver asks you to get off and walk, do it without grumbling. He will not request it unless absolutely necessary. If a team runs away, sit still and take your chances; if you jump, nine times out of ten you will be hurt.

❋ In very cold weather, abstain entirely from liquor while on the road; a man will freeze twice as quick while under its influence.

❋ Don't growl at food stations; stage companies generally provide the best they can get. Don't keep the stage waiting; many a virtuous man has lost his character by so doing.

❋ Don't smoke a strong pipe inside, especially early in the morning. Spit on the leeward side of the coach. If you have anything to take in a bottle, pass it around; a man who drinks by himself in such a case is lost to all human feeling. Provide stimulants before starting; ranch whisky is not always nectar.

❋ Don't swear, nor lop over on your neighbor when sleeping. Don't ask how far it is to the next station.

❋ Never attempt to fire a gun or pistol while on the road; it may frighten the team; and the careless handling and cocking of the weapon makes nervous people nervous.

❋ Don't discuss politics or religion, nor point out places on the road where horrible murders have been committed.

❋ Don't linger too long at the pewter wash basin at the station.

❋ Don't grease your hair before starting or dust will stick there in sufficient quantities to make a respectable 'tater' patch. Tie a silk handkerchief around your neck to keep out dust and prevent sunburns.

❋ A little glycerin is good in case of chapped hands.

❋ Don't imagine for a moment you are going on a picnic; expect annoyance, discomfort, and some hardships. If you are disappointed, thank heaven.

—*The Omaha Herald*, 1877

Respect their privacy. The Arab never speaks ill of those whose salt he has tasted; and well-bred persons will never repeat what Mrs. A. said, nor tell what Mr. A. did, when they were visiting at their house.

Remember the servants. Visitors should always give the servants who have waited upon them some little presents, either in money or its equivalent. They have had extra work in waiting upon them, and, therefore, deserve extra compensation.

The Caller

Calls cement the acquaintance with all whom you admit to your circle.

Remember the importance of calling. Formal calls in the city are intended to serve in lieu of the more genial and lengthy visits which are a part of country life. Calling is the surest way to maintain agreeable acquaintances and foster those friendships which brighten life.

Acquaint yourself with appropriate occasions for calls:

⚜ Visits of ceremony, are those which are paid after receiving attentions at the hands of your acquaintances; after dining or supping at a friend's house; after attending an evening party; etc.; and they should invariably be of short duration. One should never take either children or dogs when making them. Hand your card to the servant at the door, and ask if the lady or ladies are in. After attending a dinner party or a ball, you should call within the week upon your hostess.

⚜ Formal visits are usually paid between the hours of noon and three o'clock; informal visits at those hours when you know your friends are at leisure to receive you. It is well, in making social visits, however, not to acquire the title of a day goblin—one who, having no occupation, and delighting in the sound of his or her own voice, makes constant inroads into their friends' houses and runs in at the most unseasonable hours, saying, "Oh! it is only I, nobody minds me; let me come right up stairs."

❦ Visits of congratulation are paid after the birth of an infant, when it is also customary to send tasteful and elegant baskets or bouquets of flowers. Also, upon friends who have received an appointment to any office or dignity in the community, state, or government. If a friend has published a book, you call to congratulate him upon its success; or if he has delivered a lecture, sermon, or oration, which has elicited your applause, you call and express your high estimation of the discourse. And you pay visits of congratulation when you hear that your friends are intending to marry, and take upon themselves new responsibilities.

❦ In this world of sickness, sorrow, and bereavement, visits of condolence must occasionally be made; and, if possible, they should be paid within a week after death has entered the family circle. If your acquaintance is ceremonious, it is the custom, however, to wait until the family have appeared at church.

❦ If you have a friend who has met reverses and you desire to show your friendship by visiting her, do not go dressed expensively. Adapt your dress to her changed circumstances.

REFRAIN FROM CALLING ONLY IF YOU ARE PREPARED TO QUIT THE FRIENDSHIP. If, previous to a long voyage, or absence, or on the occasion of your marriage, you omit to call or send a card to your friends, it is understood that the acquaintance ceases. When you return home, those to whom you have sent cards, or paid visits, will pay the first visit to you.

Several Callers at Once

If when making a social call a second visitor arrives, the first caller, if she has made a call of sufficient length, should after a few minutes take her leave. When calling, if a lady find several persons have preceded her, she should invariably greet the hostess first, ignoring all others until this courtesy is shown.

—*Sloan's Cook Book and Advice to Housekeepers*, 1905

CALL AT THE PROPER TIMES. Morning calls, are not, as their title would imply, calls made in the forenoon but embrace the hours from one o' clock to five o' clock. They are generally of 15 or 20 minutes in duration. Calls in the evening are made from eight o' clock to nine o' clock and should be of an hour's duration. A gentleman whose time is his own can call between two o' clock and five o' clock. But, as business engrosses nearly all our gentlemen, from eight to half-past eight o' clock in the evening is the proper time to make a social call. If he calls before that hour, he may interfere with some previous engagement his hostess may have and will surely displease her by his eagerness. Dress suits are for evening calls.

Austin

April 5, 1891

Maggie Wilson is visiting Miss Celeste Gaylord now in S.A. All of you might call sometime. I borrow Maggie would enjoy it. She is coming over to the event. Take Mr. [?] to see her, if you can, also Mr. Graham. I would consider this a favor, for she was so nice to me. I'll enclose you a few of your cards thinking you might call and use them. I'll keep the rest for you.

—Excerpt from a letter from Winifred McCraw to her betrothed, Patrick Swearingen, in San Antonio

DEPORT YOURSELF PROPERLY DURING CALLS:

- While waiting in the parlor for the lady on whom you call to appear, the piano must remain untouched, as also the bric-a-brac.
- Sit quietly in the place the servant has assigned you, and rise

when the hostess enters. The outer wraps are retained while making calls, the brief time allowed for remaining making it unnecessary to remove them.

❈ In making a ceremonious call, a gentleman's hat and cane are retained in his hand and his gloves remain on, but an umbrella is left in the hall.

❈ Do not enter into grave discussions; trifling subjects are better.

❈ Do not draw near the fire when calling unless invited.

Many well-bred persons do not introduce their visitors to each other; but if you are left in the parlor with strangers, while the servant summons his mistress, it is not impolite to enter into conversation with them, and when the lady enters, the conversation would be mutual.

—*A Manual of Etiquette with Hints on Politeness and Good Breeding*, 1873

OVERLOOK THE PROLONGED CALL. Do not grow fidgety and anxious to make your exit if a friend with whom you call prolongs the stay longer than you desire; be composed at all times and in all places. If you are the hostess, never look at your watch; it appears as if you are desirous that they should go. The hostess does not leave the room while visitors remain.

The Correspondent

KNOW THE PURPOSES AND ETIQUETTE FOR WRITING LETTERS OF DIFFERING TYPES:

❈ Letters of introduction are used to introduce one friend to another who lives at some distance. Do not give a letter of introduction to anyone with whom you are not thoroughly acquainted. Such letters are generally left unsealed, and the name of the person introduced should be written on the lower left-hand corner of the envelope, in order that the persons on meeting may greet each other without embarrassment.

▩ Letters of friendship or letters among very intimate friends, admit of less formal terms, such as Very sincerely yours, Your dutiful son, Your affectionate nephew, etc. The chief essentials in letters of friendship are that the style be simple and the manner of expression be natural; it is the incidents of everyday life, the little things, the home chat that make a friendship letter interesting.

▩ Never write a letter when you are laboring under great excitement, for you will almost certainly write things that you will repent next day. When constrained to write severe things, the letter should be permitted to lie overnight for review before mailing. If this be done, it is probable that the character of the letter will be changed radically, or perhaps it will remain unwritten. Many letters which would seem ample provocation for a sharp reply had better go unanswered. Kind words make and hold friends, while hasty or vindictive words alienate friends.

▩ Letters of courtesy include invitations, acceptances, letters of congratulation, of condolence, of introduction, and of recommendation, all of which are more formal in style than letters of friendship.

▩ To write a good love letter you ought to begin without knowing what you are going to say and finish without knowing what you have written.

▩ To write a letter of congratulation on mourning paper is rather inconsistent.

REMEMBER THESE RULES WHEN WRITING A LETTER:

▩ In writing a letter, place the date within an inch or two of the top, at the right-hand, and be sure to write the name of the town, county, and state, with the date of the month and year; if living in a city, give the street and number also.

▩ No gentleman or lady ever writes an anonymous letter.

▩ Do not fill your letters with apologies and mere repetitions.

▩ Avoid writing with a pencil or with other than black or blue-black ink.

❈ Letters about one's own affairs, requiring an answer, should always enclose a stamp, to pay return postage.

❈ Short sentences are easier to write than long ones, hence more suitable for correspondence.

❈ The signature should be written very plainly, for no matter how familiar your intimate friends are with your dashing ink lines, others may have considerable difficulty in associating them with your printed name.

❈ In social correspondence, the envelopes, like the paper, should be white and plain, and should correspond to the paper used in size and quality. It is considered bad taste to use colored paper, or other than black ink.

❈ Be sure to write to a friend, or hostess, after making a visit at her house, thanking her for her hospitality. Don't wait a fortnight before doing so.

❈ It is the fault of the English language that we have so many "bad spellers." If you are doubtful of a word, it will be better to look it up rather than make a blot, or a running line, where the letters are questioned. Careful reading, and lots of it, will make a good speller.

Chapter Eighteen

For the Lady in Mourning

Mourning Practices

Follow these guidelines for mourning:

🦋 A widow's mourning should last 18 months. The color of black for heavy mourning should be a dull dead hue, not a blue-black nor yet with any brown shade. For the first six months, the dress should be of crape cloth or Henrietta cloth covered entirely with crape, collar and cuffs of white crape, a crape bonnet with a long crape veil, and a widow's cap of white crape if preferred. After six months' mourning, the crape can be removed and grenadine trimmings used, if the smell of crape is offensive, as it is to some people. After 12 months, the widow's cap is left off and the heavy veil is exchanged for a lighter one. The dress can be of silk grenadine, plain black gros grain, or crape-trimmed cashmere with jet trimmings, and crepe lisse about the neck and sleeves. Bows, flowers, and decorative finishing generally are wholly out of place in deep mourning; lace and embroidery are wholly inadmissible.

🦋 The veil is always of crape and in this country is worn very long—most inconveniently and absurdly so, indeed. This fashion is very much objected to by doctors, who think many diseases of the eye come by this means. The crape also sheds its pernicious dye into the sensitive nostrils, producing catarrhal disease as well as blindness and cataract of the eye. It is a thousand pities that fashion dictates the crape veil, but so it is. It is the very banner of woe, and no one has the courage to go without it. We can only suggest to mourners wearing it that they should pin a small veil of black tulle over the eyes and nose and throw back the heavy crape as often as possible, for health's sake.

❧ Mourning for a father or mother should last one year. A deep veil is worn at the back of the bonnet, but not over the head or face like the widow's veil, which covers the entire person when down. Mourning for a brother or sister, for stepfather or stepmother, and for grandparents may be the same as for the parents, but the duration may be shorter.

❧ The period of mourning for an aunt or uncle or cousin is of three months' duration.

❧ Wives and husbands wear mourning for relatives of their spouses.

❧ Mourning for children should last nine months. In the first three months, the dress should be crape-trimmed, the mourning less deep than that for a husband. No one is ever ready to take off mourning; therefore these rules have this advantage—they enable the friends around a grief-stricken mother to tell her when is the time to make her dress more cheerful, which she is bound to do for the sake of the survivors, many of whom are perhaps affected for life by seeing a mother always in black. It is well for mothers to remember this when sorrow for a lost child makes all the earth seem barren to them.

Funeral Etiquette

DRESS THE DECEASED SIMPLY. In dressing the remains for the grave, those of a man are usually "clad in his habit as he lived." For a woman, tastes differ; a white robe and cap, not necessarily shroud-like, are decidedly unexceptionable. For young persons and children, white cashmere robes and flowers are always most appropriate.

USE FLOWERS SPARINGLY. A few flowers placed in the dead hand—perhaps a simple wreath—is plenty, but not those unmeaning memorials which have become to real mourners such sad perversities of good taste and such a misuse of flowers. Let those who can afford to send such things devote the money to the use of poor mothers who cannot afford to buy a coffin for a dead child or a coat for a living one.

He took me to none of the costly monuments, nor graves of famous folk, but wandered here and there among the trees, his hands clasped behind him, stopping now and then at a green mound, while he told me curious fragments of the life which was ended below. He mentioned no names—they would have meant nothing to me if he had—but he wrested the secret meaning out of each life, pouncing on it, holding it up with a certain racy enjoyment in his own astuteness. . . . I must confess that I think he forgot the country and its homage and me that morning, and talked simply for his own pleasure in his own pathos and fun, just as a woman might take out her jewels when she was alone, to hold up the glittering strings and take delight in their shining. Once, I remember, he halted by a magnificent shaft and read the bead roll of the virtues of the man who lay beneath: "A devoted husband, a tender father, a noble citizen—dying triumphant in the Christian faith."

"Now this dead man," he said, in a high, rasping tone, "was a prize fighter, a drunkard, and a thief. He beat his wife. But she puts up this stone. He had money!"

Then he hurried me across the slopes to an obscure corner where a grave was hidden by high, wild grasses. He knelt and parted the long branches. Under them was a little headstone with the initials "M. H.," and underneath the verse:

She lived unknown and few could know
When Mary ceased to be, but she is gone, and Oh!
The difference to me!

—"Bits of Gossip," 1904

Follow proper practice when death is caused by disease. Bodies of persons dying of smallpox, scarlet fever, diphtheria, membranous croup, or measles should be wrapped in several thicknesses of cloth wrung out of full-strength corrosive sublimate, carbolic, or formaldehyde solution and should not thereafter be exposed. The funeral should be private and no persons except the undertaker and his assistant, the clergyman, and the immediate family of the deceased should attend. Carriages used by persons attending the funeral ceremony should be fumigated. No person should enter the sick room until it has been thoroughly disinfected.

Prevent burying a loved one alive. Since there are no reliable methods for determining death and since new chemical and industrial methods of putting people in comas are multiplying in society, the fear of burial alive is very real. There have been reports of corpses exhumed with hair and nails grown long and fingernail scratches in the coffin lid. The reader is directed to a recently patented improved burial case. The nature of this invention consists in placing on the lid of the coffin, and directly over the face of the body laid therein, a square tube, which extends from the coffin up through and over the surface of the grave, said tube containing a ladder and a cord, one end of said cord being placed in the hand of the person laid in the coffin, and the other end of said cord being attached to a bell on the top of the square tube; so that, should a person be interred ere life is extinct, he can, on recovery to consciousness, ascend from the grave and the coffin by the ladder; or, if not able to ascend by said ladder, ring the bell, thereby giving an alarm, and thus save himself from premature burial and death; and if, on inspection, life is extinct, the tube is withdrawn, the sliding door closed, and the tube used for a similar purpose.

# BIBLIOGRAPHY

Books and Articles

American Stove Co., Publishers. *Cook Book: "New Process" Wick Oil Cook Stove*. American Stove Co., Publishers, ca. 1910. At: Emergence of Advertising in America: 1850–1920 (see websites).

Ames, John. "Leaving Texas." *Overland Monthly and Out West Magazine*, Vol. 12, Issue 2, February 1874. At: Making of America (see websites).

Barr, Amelia E. *Remember the Alamo*. New York: Dodd, Mead, and Company, 1888. At: A Celebration of Women's Writers (see websites).

California Fruit Growers Exchange, Publishers. *Recipes for Dainty Dishes: Culinary Toilet, and Medicinal Hints*. California Fruit Growers Exchange, ca. 1910s. At: Emergence of Advertising in America: 1850–1920 (see websites).

Cary, Phoebe. "The Two Lovers." *Appletons' Journal: A Magazine of General Literature*, Vol. 5, Issue 102, March 11, 1871. At: Making of America (see websites).

Chase, A.W., M.D. *Dr. Chase's Third Last and Complete Receipt Book and Household Physician (Memorial Edition)*. Detroit: F.B. Dickerson Company, 1903.

Church & Dwight Co., Publishers. *Cow Brand Soda Cook Book and Facts Worth Knowing, Established Half a Century*. New York: Church & Dwight Co., 1900. At: Emergence of Advertising in America: 1850–1920 (see websites).

C. I. Hood & Co. Apothecaries, Publishers. *Hood's Cook Book Reprint Number One.* Lowell, MA: C. I. Hood & Co., post 1877. At: Emergence of Advertising in America: 1850–1920 (see websites).

Clifford, Josephine. "To Texas, And By the Way." *Overland Monthly and Out West Magazine,* Vol. 7, Issue 3, September 1871. At: Making of America (see websites).

Cooper, Sarah B. "Ideal Womanhood." *Overland Monthly and Out West Magazine,* Vol. 7, Issue 4, October 1871. At: Making of America (see websites).

Coolidge, Susan. *What Katy Did.* Boston: Roberts Brothers, 1887. At: A Celebration of Women's Writers (see websites).

Corson, Juliet. *Miss Corson's Practical American Cookery and Household Management.* New York: Dodd, Mead, and Company, 1885.

D. Ransom Son & Co., Publishers. *Ransom's Family Receipt Book.* Buffalo, NY: D. Ransom Son & Co., 1885. At: Emergence of Advertising in America: 1850–1920 (see websites).

Davis, Rebecca Harding. *Bits of Gossip.* Boston and New York: Houghton, Mifflin & Company and Cambridge: The Riverside Press, 1904. At: University of North Carolina's Documenting the American South Collection (see websites).

Drew, Grace E. "Art and Fashion in Dinner-Giving." *Godey's Lady's Book,* December 1896. At: Godey's Lady's Book On-Line (see websites).

Farmer, Fannie Merritt. *Catering for Special Occasions.* Philadelphia: David McKay, 1911.

Farmer, Fannie Merritt. *The Boston Cooking-School Cook Book.* Boston: Little, Brown, and Company, 1896. Reprint, Mineola, NY: Dover Publications, Inc., 1997.

"Fashions in Calling Cards," *Harper's Bazar,* 1868. At: Victoriana.Com Study Center (see websites).

First Baptist Church Cookbook, 1909. Cited in: Taste from the First: 1989 Centennial of First Baptist Church of Amarillo, Texas. Amarillo, Texas: First Baptist Church, 1989.

French, Celia M. "Aunt Sally's Home." *Ladies' Repository: A Monthly Periodical, Devoted to Literature, Arts, and Religion,* Vol. 11, Issue 2. Cincinnati: Methodist Episcopal Church, 1873. At: Making of America (see websites).

Galwey, T.F. "Among the Insects in a Southern City." *Catholic World,* Vol. 41, Issue 244, July 1885. At: Making of America (see websites).

Gillette, Mrs. F.L., and Hugo Ziemann. *The White House Cook Book.* Chicago: The Werner Company, 1887. Reprint, Ottenheimer Publishers, Inc., 1999.

Haliburton, Thomas Chandler and Sam Slick [pseud.]. *The Letter-Bag of the Great Western.* New York: G. Routledge and Sons, 1873. At Making of America (see websites).

Hammond, S. H. and L. W. Mansfield. *Country Margins and Rambles of a Journalist,* New York: J.C. Derby, 1855. At: The On-Line Books Page (see websites).

Harland, Marion. *Common Sense in the Household: A Manual of Practical Housewifery.* New York: Charles Scribner & Co., 1871.

Hayes, Rutherford B. White House Diary Entry, March 18, 1878. At: The Ohio Historical Society (see websites).

Healy & Bigelow, Publishers. *Healy & Bigelow's New Cook Book.* New Haven, CT: Healy & Bigelow, 1890. At: Emergence of Advertising in America: 1850–1920 (see websites).

Henry, O. "Last of the Troubadours." *Everybody's Magazine,* July, 1908.

"Hints for Plains Travelers," *Omaha Herald,* 1877. At: Wells Fargo (see websites).

Huntington, Emily. *The Cooking Garden: A Systematized Course of Cooking for Pupils of All Ages, Including Plan of Work, Bills of Fare, Songs, and Letters of Information.* New York: Trow's Printing and Bookbinding Company, 1885.

International Health Resort, Publishers. *International Health Resort Recipes.* Chicago: International Health Resort, ca. 1900. At: Emergence of Advertising in America: 1850–1920 (see websites).

J.D. Larkin & Co., Publishers. *Sweet Home Cook Book.* Buffalo, NY: 1888. Reprint, Paducah, KY: Image Graphics, Inc.

Jeffries, Prof. B.G., and J.L. Nichols. *The Household Guide or Domestic Cyclopedia.* Naperville, IL: J.L. Nichols & Co., 1898.

Jeremiah Curtis & Sons and John I. Brown & Sons, Publishers. *Mrs. Winslow's Domestic Receipt Book.* Boston: Jeremiah Curtis & Sons and London: John I. Brown & Sons, 1877. At: Emergence of Advertising in America: 1850–1920 (see websites).

Johnson, Helen Louise. *The Enterprising Housekeeper, Suggestions for Breakfast, Luncheon, and Supper 2nd ed.* Philadelphia: The Enterprise Manufacturing Co., 1898. At: Emergence of Advertising in America: 1850–1920 (see websites).

Kander, Mrs. Simon and Mrs. Henry Schoenfeld. *The Way to a Man's Heart.* Milwaukee: The Milwaukee Settlement House, 1903. Reprint, *The Settlement Cook Book.* Bedford, MA: Applewood Books, 1996.

Kearney, Belle. *A Slaveholder's Daughter.* New York: The Abbey Press, ca. 1900. At: Documenting the American South (see websites).

Keary, A. E., and M. *Enchanted Tulips and Other Verses for Children.* London: Macmillan and Co., 1914. At: A Celebration of Women's Writers (see websites).

Ladies Association of The First Presbyterian Church, Houston, Texas. *The First Texas Cookbook,* 1883. Reprint, *The First Texas Cookbook-A Thorough Treatise on the Art of Cookery in 1883.* Austin, TX: Eakin Publications, Inc., 1986.

Lincoln, Mrs. Mary J., Lida Ames Willis, Mrs. Sarah Tyson Rorer, Mrs. Helen Armstrong, and Marion Harland. *Home Helps, A Pure Food Cook Book A Useful Collection of Up-to-Date, Practical Recipes by Five of the Leading Culinary Experts in the United States.* Chicago, New York, St. Louis, New Orleans, and Montreal: The N.K. Fairbank Company, 1910. At: Emergence of Advertising in America: 1850–1920 (see websites).

Logan, Olive (Mrs. Wirt Sikes). *Get thee behind me, Satan! A home-born book of home-truths.* New York: Adams, Victor & Co., 1872. At: Making of America (see websites).

Mallon, Isabel A. "The Small Belongings of Dress." *The Ladies' Home Journal,* April 1894. At: The Costume Gallery (see websites).

McCraw, Winifred. Letters to Patrick Henry Swearingen, April 1, 1891; April 3, 1891; April 5, 1891. Winifred McCraw and Patrick Henry Swearingen Papers, Winifred McCraw Series, Box 1, Folder 9. Special Collections and Archives Department, University of Texas at San Antonio Libraries.

Michigan Stove Company, Publishers. *Cupid at Home in the Kitchen.* Detroit and Chicago: The Michigan Stove Company, ca. 1910. At: Emergence of Advertising in America: 1850-1920 (see websites).

Miss Beecher's Housekeeper and Healthkeeper: Containing Five Hundred Recipes for Economical and Healthful Cooking; also *Many Directions for Securing Health and Happiness.* New York: Harper & Brothers, Publishers, 1873. At: Making of America (see websites).

Myers, Mrs. E. G. *The Capitol Cook Book, a Selection of Tested Recipes, by the Ladies of Albert Sidney Johnston Chapter, Daughters of the Confederacy.* Austin, TX: Van Boeckmann, Schutze & Company, Printers, 1899. Reprint, *The Capitol Cookbook, a Facsimile of the Austin 1899 Edition.* Austin, TX: State House Press, 1995.

Natural Food Company, Publishers. *The Vital Question Cook Book, The "Vital Question" Being a Discussion of the Food Problem and its Relation to Health and Happiness Including a Comprehensive Treatise on the Principles of Cookery with Practical and Economical Recipes for Making Simple, Palatable and Nutritious Shredded Wheat Dishes.* Niagara Falls, NY: 1908. At: Emergence of Advertising in America: 1850-1920 (see websites).

O'Rell, Max. "Studies in Cheerfulness–I." *The North American Review,* Vol. 167, Issue 505, December, 1898. Cedar Falls, IA: University of Northern Iowa.

"Our New Cook Book," *Peterson's Magazine,* Vol. LIII, No. 3, March 1868. At: Victoriana.Com Study Center (see websites).

P.O.E. Cook Book: Souvenir Edition. Knoxville, IA: Curis & Gibson, 1908. Reprint, David E. Schoonover. Iowa City: University of Iowa Press, 1992.

Powers, Stephen. "Solid Days in Texas." *Overland Monthly and Out West Magazine,* Vol. 6, Issue 6, June 1871. At: Making of America (see websites).

Price Flavoring Extract Co., Publishers. *Dr. Price's Delicious Desserts.* Chicago: Price Flavoring Extract Co., 1904. At: Emergence of Advertising in America: 1850-1920 (see websites).

Rees, James. *The Life of Edwin Forrest.* With reminiscences and personal recollections. T. B. Peterson & Brothers, 1874. At: Making of America (see websites).

Rorer, Sarah Tyson. *Cereal Foods and How to Cook Them.* Chicago: American Cereal Company, 1899. At: Emergence of Advertising in America: 1850–1920 (see websites).

Sears, Roebuck and Co., Publishers. *"Kook Kwick" Pressure Cooker Recipes.* Sears, Roebuck and Co., ca. 1910s. At: Emergence of Advertising in America: 1850–1920 (see websites).

Seely, Mrs. L. *Mrs. Seely's Cook Book: A Manual of French and American Cookery.* New York: The MacMillan Company, 1902.

Sloan, Dr. Earl S. *Sloan's Cook Book and Advice to Housekeepers* (Recipes and Advertisements for Remedies Manufactured by Dr. Earl S. Sloan at 615 Albany Street and 111 East Brookline Street, Boston). Boston: F. E. Bacon & Co. Printers, 1905. At: Emergence of Advertising in America: 1850–1920 (see websites).

Stoddard, Elizabeth. "The Tea-Party." *Appletons Journal: A Magazine of General Literature,* Vol. 6, Issue 132, October 7, 1871. New York: D. Appleton and Company. At: Making of America (see websites).

Stopes, Marie C. *Married Love.* London: G.P. Putnam Sons, 1918. At: A Celebration of Women's Writers (see websites).

Stowe, Harriet Beecher. *House and Home Papers.* Boston: Fields, Osgood, & Co, 1869. At: Making of America (see websites).

"Styles of the Month for Children," *McCall's Magazine,* Vol. XXXV, No. 9, May 1908. At: The Costume Gallery (see websites).

Swift & Company, Publishers. *The Kitchen Encyclopedia.* Swift & Company, 1911. At: Emergence of Advertising in America: 1850–1920 (see websites).

"Teaching Table Manners," *The Ladies' Repository: A Monthly Periodical, Devoted to Literature, Arts, and Religion,* Vol. 25, Issue 2, February, 1865. Cincinnati: Methodist Episcopal Church. At: Making of America (see websites).

Tyree, Marion Cabell. *Housekeeping in Old Virginia.* Louisville, KY: John P. Morton & Co., 1879.

Vollrath Co., Publishers. *Cuisine*. Wisconsin: Vollrath Co., 1912. At: Emergence of Advertising in America: 1850–1920 (see websites).

Wallace, Lily Haxworth. *The Rumford Complete Cook Book*. Providence, RI: Rumford Chemical Works, 1908.

What Mrs. Fisher Knows About Old Southern Cooking: Soups, Pickles, Preserves, Etc. San Francisco: Women's Co-operative Printing Office, 1881. Reprint, with historical notes by Karen Hess. Bedford, MA: Applewood Books, 1995.

W. M. Underwood Co., Publishers. *Taste the Taste and Some Cookery News*. Boston: W. M. Underwood Co., ca 1910. At: Emergence of Advertising in America: 1850–1920 (see websites).

Women of the First Congregational Church of Marysville, Ohio. *Centennial Buckeye Cook Book*. Marysville, OH: J.H. Shearer & Son, 1876. Reprint, *Centennial Buckeye Cook Book Originally Published in 1876,* with an introduction and appendices by Andrew F. Smith, Columbus: Ohio State University Press, 2000.

Wood-Allen, M.D., Mary and Sylvanus Stall, D.D. *What a Young Woman Ought to Know*. Philadelphia and London: The Vir Publishing Company, 1898.

Wright, A.S. *Wright's Book of 3,000 Practical Receipts*. New York: Dick & Fitzgerald, 1869. At: Making of America (see websites).

Wright, Mrs. D. Giraud. *A Southern Girl in '61—The War-Time Memories of a Confederate Senator's Daughter*. New York: Doubleday, Page & Co., 1905. At: Documenting the American South (see websites).

Websites

A Celebration of Women Writers
digital.library.upenn.edu/women/writers.html

The Costume Gallery   www.costumegallery.com

Emergence of Advertising in America: 1850–1920 Cookbook Collection
http://scriptorium.lib.duke.edu/eaa/

Godey's Lady's Book   www.spiritone.com

Making of America Project
   moa.umdl.umich.edu or moa.cit.cornell.edu/moa/index.html

The Ohio Historical Society   www.ohiohistory.org

The On-Line Books Page   digital.library.upenn.edu/books

University of North Carolina at Chapel Hill Libraries Documenting the American South Collection   docsouth.unc.edu/southlit/southlit.html

Victoriana.Com Study Center   www.victoriana.com

Wells Fargo   www.wellsfargo.com

 # INDEX

Abortion, 81–82
Accessories, 16
Afternoon teas, 190
"Among the Insects in a Southern City" (Gawley), 99
Animal care/maintenance, 108–110
Apple Fritters recipe, 175
Apple Lemon Pudding recipe, 179
Appletons' Journal (1871), 14, 30, 34, 68, 69
"The Arm Chair" *(Enchanted Tulips and Other Verses for Children)*, 88
Arrowroot recipe, 48–49
"Aunt Sally's Home" *(Ladies' Repository)*, 61
Austrian Coffee for Teas and Receptions recipe, 186
Autumn dinner desserts, 178

Barbecued Fish recipe, 151
Barn
  care of animals in, 108–110
  miscellaneous receipts for animals in, 111–112
Barr, Amelia E., 23
Bathing
  using cold water for, 6
  with rain water, 6
  weekly, 5
Bedbugs, 94
Beefsteak Pie recipe, 170–171
Beverage recipes, 117, 181–184
Bicycle mount, 29
A Bishop recipe, 183

Bisque Soup recipe, 166
"Bits of Gossip" (1904), 211
Bodice, 17
Bonnets, 16
Boston Cooking-School Cook Book (1896), 142, 194
Bracelets, 16
Bread
  most economical breakfast dish using, 148
  preparing, 113–116
  recipes for cereals and, 141–148
  uses for stale, 147
Breakfast dishes
  Hamburg Steak recipe, 152
  most economical, 148
  recipes for, 141–148
Breakfast menus, 142
Breakfast tea, 144
Broiled Tomatoes recipe, 155
Burial practices, 212
Burn treatments
  gunpowder burns, 71
  recipe for scald, 72
Butter churning/management, 118–119
Buttermilk, 183

Calf's Head Soup recipe, 166–167
Calling etiquette, 203–206
The Capitol Cookbook (1899), 18, 73, 91, 115, 116, 151, 155, 166, 167, 175, 187
Cary, Phoebe, 30, 34, 68

[221]

Catering for Special Occasions (1911), 174, 177, 185, 188, 191
Catholic World (1885), 99
Centennial Buckeye Cookbook (1876), 11 15, 20, 163, 194
Cereal Foods and How to Cook Them (1899), 144, 181
Cereal recipes, 141–148
Charlotte Russe recipe, 175
Cheese and egg recipes, 158–160
Chestnut salad recipe, 161
Chicken Gumbo No. 2 recipe, 166
Chicken Lunch for Traveling recipe, 198
Chicken Salad recipe, 162–163
Childbirth preparation recipes, 80–81
Childrearing
  avoid fault-finding while, 61–62
  clothing
    sleepware, 44
    thoughts on, 49–51
  parental example in, 59–60
  playtime advice, 51–54
  praise and punishment used in, 60–62
  rules for sleep, 43–45
  rules for their diets
    for little ones under three, 46–48
    overview of, 45–46
    recipes for nursery, 48–49
  See also Mothers
Children
  miscellaneous recipes for sick, 55–57
  rules for deportment of, 64–65
  treatment of jaundice in, 57
  treatment to prevent rickets in, 58
Childrens Repository, 66
Chili Con Carne with Frijoles recipe, 149
Chocolate Tarts recipe, 176
Chow-Chow recipe, 164
Christmas Dinner menu, 194
Cleaning. *See* Recipes (household)
Clifford, Josephine, 28, 85
Clothing
  for children
    sleepware, 44
    thoughts on, 49–51
  guidelines
    on adding accessories, 16
    on bonnets, 16
    on corsets, 18
  mending, 14–15
  mourning etiquette and, 209–210
  overview of, 13–18
  recipes for care of, 19
  recommendation for washing, 20
Cocoa recipe, 181
Coffee recipes, 117, 181, 184, 186
Cold prevention, 78
Colicky babies, 55
Cologne water recipe, 8
Common Sense in the Household (1871), 146, 176, 192
Constipation remedy, 74
Conversation etiquette, 22–25
Cook Book: "New Process" Wick Oil Cook Stove (1910s), 154, 156, 157
Cooking Garden (1885), 147, 166
Cooking measurements, 138–139
Cooking tasks
  daily, 135–136
  using food colors for, 134
  household measures used for, 138–140
  preparing common foods
    breads, 113–116
    common meats and game, 120–123
    desserts, 132–134
    fish, 126–128
    milk and butter, 117–120
    pork, 123–125
    seasonings and relishes, 130–132
    tea and coffee, 116–117
    terrapin and green turtle, 125–126
    vegetables, 128–130
  seasonal, 136–138
  See also Recipes (cooking)
Corn and Cheese Soufflé recipe, 156
Corn Meal Mush recipe, 142–143
Correspondence etiquette, 206–208
Corsets, 18
Cosmetic recipes, 10–12
Cottage Pudding recipe, 174
Cough remedies, 56–57
Cough remedy, 77

Courting etiquettes of girls
  advice to parents of girls regarding, 33
  for ladies and gentlemen, 30–33
  regarding marriage proposals, 34–35
Cow Brand Soda Cook Book and Facts Worth Knowing (1900), 114
Crackling Bread recipe, 146
Cream Fritters recipe, 144
Creams
  recipes for dressing table, 10–12
  recipes for skin and face, 8–10
Cream Slaw recipe, 163
Croup remedies, 55–56
Crullers recipe, 147
Cuisine (1912), 172
Cupid at Home in the Kitchen (1910s), 176

Daily cooking tasks, 135–136
Dancing etiquette, 29
Demeanor
  during calls, 205–206
  in social exchanges, 22–25
  on the street, 25–26
  See also Etiquette
Desserts
  preparation of, 132–134
  recipes for, 173–180
  for spring teas or luncheons, 187
  for summer and autumn dinners, 178
Dining room furnishings, 88–91
Dinner menus, 168
Disease. *See* Illness
Domestic animals
  care of, 108–110
  miscellaneous receipts for, 111–112
Domestic wisdom
  on childrearing
    on diets, 45–49
    discontented babies, 54–55
    on dressing, 49–51
    regarding playtime, 51–54
    sick children, 55–58
    on sleeping arrangements, 43–45
  financial, 41
  on hostess duties, 195–198
  on illnesses and remedies

    adults, 70–79
    children and, 54–57
    legacy of 19th century Texas women's, 1–3
    regarding causes of abortion, 81–82
    regarding childbirth, 80–81
    for wives, 37–42
  See also Cooking tasks
Dr. Chase's Third Last and Complete Receipt Book and Household Physician (1903), 57, 70, 71, 76, 82, 163, 172, 177, 179, 192, 193
Dressing table creams/cosmetics, 10–12
Dr. Price's Delicious Desserts (1904), 134, 178, 180
Dr. Price's Ice Cream Sugar recipe, 180
Dutch or Pot Cheese recipe, 158
Dysentery remedy, 74
Dyspepsia
  preventing, 74–75
  remedy for, 76–77

Easter eggs, 120
Eggs
  preparation of, 119–120
  prepared for Easter, 120
  recipes for cheese and, 158–160
Eggs in Disguise recipe, 159
Enchanted Tulips and Other Verses for Children (1914), 53, 63, 88
Enemies, 24–25
Engagement, 35
English Monkey recipe, 160
The Enterprising Housekeeper (1889), 3, 155, 164
Escorting ladies, 27–30
Etiquette
  calling, 203–206
  conversation, 22–25
  correspondence, 206–208
  courting, 30–33
  dancing, 29
  for marriage proposals, 34–35
  mourning, 209–212
  during social exchanges, 22–25
  while walking on street, 25–26
  for wearing jewelry, 16

Etiquette *(continued)*
    when being escorted, 27–30
    while visiting/traveling, 199–203
    See also Demeanor
Excellent Light Biscuits recipe, 145
Exercises, 8

Face care recipes, 8–10
Farms
    care of animals in, 108–110
    miscellaneous receipts for animals on, 111–112
Fault-finding, 61–62
Financial advice, 41
Fine Cottage Cheese recipe, 159
First Baptist Church Cookbook (1907), 142
First Texas Cookbook, 143, 147, 158, 163
Fish
    preparation of, 126–128
    recipes for, 151–152
Five O'clock Tea recipe, 185
Floating Island recipe, 183
Food coloring, 134
Fourth of July Punch recipe, 191
Freckles remover, 10
French, Celia M., 61
Fricandelles recipe, 151
Fricasseed Chicken recipe, 170
Fricassee of Veal recipe, 170
Fried Bread (or Egg Toast) recipe, 146
Friendships
    calling etiquette and, 204
    encouraging children's, 53
Frijoles recipe, 154
Front room furnishings, 86–87
Funeral flowers, 211

Galloway, Sam, 143
Game preparation, 120–123
Gardens
    children and, 53
    creating and maintaining, 105–107
Gawley, T. F., 99
Gentlemen
    courting etiquette for, 30–33
    dancing etiquette for, 29
    escorting ladies, 27–30

Get Thee Behind Me, Satan! A Home-Born Book of Home-Truths (1872), 33, 38
Ginger, 78
Ginger Snaps recipe, 177
Gloves, 7
Godey's Lady's Book, 2
Gold or Silver Cake recipe, 186
Gossip, 24
Graham Hasty Pudding recipe, 49
Grandpa's Favorite Griddle Cakes recipe, 145–146
Gray hair prevention, 12
Green Gooseberry Tart recipe, 188
Green turtle preparation, 125–126
Grooming
    advice for the married woman, 39
    bathing, 5–7
    daily teeth cleaning, 7, 13
    good nutrition as part of, 7–8
    guidelines for, 5–8
    protecting hands with gloves, 7
    recipes
        for hair, 12
        for skin and face, 8–12
        for teeth, 12–13
    suitable exercises as part of, 8
Guests
    preparing luncheon for their departure, 198
    receiving your husband's, 195–196
    in your home, 196–198
Gunpowder burns treatment, 71

Hair-curling liquid, 12
Hair grooming
    recipes for, 12
    tips on, 13
    washing, 7
Hamburg Steak for Breakfast or Supper recipe, 152
Ham preparation, 124–125
Hand care recipes, 8–10
Harper's Bazaar, 2
Harper's New Monthly Magazine (1868), 52
Hayes, Rutherford B., 152
Hayson, A. G., 70

[224]

Headache cure, 74
Healy & Bigelow's New Cook Book (1890), 58, 158, 183
Hecker's Farina recipe, 48
Hermits recipe, 176
Hog's Head Cheese recipe, 158
Holiday recipes, 191–194
Home furnishing/decorating
   cleaning/polishing utensils and, 94–96
   the dining room, 88–91
   the front room, 86–87
   general information on, 83–85
   kitchen, 97–104
   sleeping rooms, 92–93
Home Helps (1910), 143, 145, 155, 156, 157
Honeymoon days, 36
Honor Sandwiches for St. Valentine's Tea recipe, 190
Hood's Cook Book Reprint Number One (1877), 9, 75, 151
Hood's Olive Ointment, 9
Horseback mount, 28
Hostess duties
   for guests in your home, 196–198
   preparing luncheon for departing guests, 198
   receiving husband's guests, 195–196
Hot Coffee and Soda recipe, 184
Household
   arranging kitchen in, 97–104
   care of domestic animals, 108–110
   creating/maintaining garden for, 105–107
   furnishing and decorating, 83–96
   remedies for pests in, 93–94
   treatment of guests in your, 195–198
   See also Recipes (household)
The Household Guide (1902), 7
Household receipts
   cleaning/polishing furniture and utensils, 94–96
   household pests remedies, 93–94
House and Home Papers (Stowe), 119, 121, 122, 144, 182, 186
"Housekeeper's Alphabet," 83–84
Housekeeping in Old Virginia (1879), 181

Ice cream, 133–134, 180
"Ideal Womanhood" *(Overland Monthly and Out West Magazine)*, 36
Illness
   benefits of Texas climate to, 70
   causes of abortion, 81–82
   mourning practice for death caused by, 212
   nursing of patients due to, 67–69
   recipes
      for adult, 70–78
      for discontented babies, 54–55
      for other conditions/cures, 78–79
      preparation for childbirth, 80–81
      for sick children, 55–57
   See also Sick room
International Health Resort Recipes (1900s), 161, 190
Italian Salad recipe, 161

Jam Jumbles recipe, 187–188
Jaundice treatment, 57
Jewelry etiquette, 16

Kickpoo Indian Remedies, 58
Kissing etiquette, 25
Kitchen
   characteristics of a Southern, 99
   furniture in, 97–100
   storeroom in, 103–104
   useful objects to have in, 100–102
The Kitchen Encyclopedia (1911), 171
"Kook Kwick" Pressure Cooker Recipes (1910s), 170

The Ladies Repository, 2, 61
Ladies. See 19th century Texas women
Lady caller etiquette, 203–206
Lady correspondent, 206–208
Lady Fingers recipe, 176–177
Lady as hostess, 195–198
Lady in mourning, 209–212
Lady visitor, 199–202
"Last of the Troubadours" (1908), 143
Laughter, 24
"Leaving Texas" (1874), 117, 118
Leg of Mutton Stuffed recipe, 172

Lemonade, 78
The Letter-Bag of the Great Western (1873), 108
Letter-writing etiquette, 206–208
Lobster à la Newburg recipe, 169
Loving Cup recipe, 182
Luncheons
  desserts for, 187
  menus for, 150
  recipes for special occasion, 185–190

Macaroni Casserole recipe, 153–154
McCall's Magazine (1908), 50
McCraw, Winifred, 17, 87, 109, 205
Manners cultivation, 21–22
  See also Etiquette
A Manual of Etiquette with Hints on Politeness and Good Breeding (1873), 22, 29, 41, 206
Marriage
  advice for wives, 37–42
  etiquette for proposal of, 34–35
Married Love (1918), 39, 40, 42
Meats
  preparation of common, 120–123
  recipes for dinner, 169–172
  recipes for, 149–153
  serving fresh, 121
Menus
  breakfast, 142
  Christmas Dinner, 194
  dinner, 168
  luncheon, 150
  summer, 163
  supper, 155
Milk
  buttermilk, 183
  management of butter and, 117–118
Miss Beecher's Housekeeper and Healthkeeper (1873), 110, 148, 159, 179, 183
Mistletoe, 78–79
Mock Oysters recipe, 157
Mock Turtle Soup recipe, 167
Mothers
  home instruction by
    on children's deportment, 64–65
    overview of, 62–64
  parental example of, 59–60
  use of praise and punishment, 60–62
  See also Childrearing; Wives
Mourning etiquette, 209–212
Mrs. Seely's Cook Book (1902), 186
Mrs. Winslow's Domestic Receipt Book (1878), 149

Nausea remedy, 74
19th century Texas women
  as center of family, 1
  courting
    etiquette while being, 30–33
    proposal during, 34–35
  cultivating personal carriage/grace, 21–22
  demeanor
    during social exchanges, 22–25
    on the street, 25–26
  escorting, 27–30
  grooming guidelines/recipes for, 5–13, 39
  guidelines for dressing, 13–19
  as hostess, 195–198
  lady visitor, caller, correspondent roles of, 199–208
  mourning etiquette for, 209–212
  suitable exercises for, 8
  See also Domestic wisdom; Mothers; Wives
Nursing practices, 67–69
Nutmeg, 79
Nutrition
  guidelines on children's, 45–49
  importance of good, 7–8

Oatmeal toilet soap, 11
Olla Podrida recipe, 154–155
The Omaha Herald (1877), 202
Onions (mashed and raw), 79
Orange juice, 79
Orange Salad recipe, 160
Outdoor sleeping arrangements, 93
Out West Magazine (1871), 28, 36, 77, 85
Overland Monthly (1871), 28, 36, 77, 85
Oyster Pie recipe, 152

Pampering your body, 6–7
Parental example, 59–60
Parsley seeds, 78
Passionflower, 79
Peach Tapioca Pudding recipe, 177
Peanut Drops recipe, 174
Pearl Wheat or Cracked Wheat recipe, 148
Pea Soup recipe, 166
Personal carriage, 21–22
Peterson's Magazine (1868), 182
Pickles/pickling, 131–132
Pineapple Bavarian Cream recipe, 173
Playtime advice, 51–54
Plum puddings, 134
"Plum Pudding to Englishmen's Taste, in Rhyme" *(Dr. Chase's…)*, 179
P.O.F. Cook Book: Souvenir Edition (1908), 165
Popovers recipe, 145
Pork preparation, 123–125
Potato Dressing recipe, 193
Potatoes à la Maître d'Hôtel recipe, 156–157
Potatoes in Seven Ways for Dinner recipes, 171–172
Potato Yeast Bread recipe, 143
Poultry raising, 110
Powers, Hiram, 18
Powers, Stephen, 77
Practical American Cookery (1885), 145, 184
Praise and punishment, 60–62
Professor Gunn's Treatment for Burns from Gunpowder, 71
Pudding Sauces recipes, 174–175
Pumpkin Pie recipe, 192

Ransom's Family Receipt Book (1885), 170
"Recipe for Good Temper" *(Centennial Buckeye Cookbook)*, 15
Recipes (cooking)
 beverages, 117, 181–184
 bread and cereals, 141–148
 desserts, 173–180
 eggs and cheese, 158–160
 fish, 151–152
 luncheon for departing guests, 198
 meats, 149–153
 salad, 160–164
 soups, 165–167
 special occasions
  holidays, 191–194
  teas and luncheons, 185–190
 vegetables, 153–158
 See also Cooking tasks
Recipes for Dainty Dishes: Culinary Toilet and Medicinal Hints (1910), 10, 160, 190
Recipes (household)
 cleaning/polishing furniture and utensils, 94–96
 clothing care, 19
 for domestic animal care, 111–112
 grooming care
  for hair, 12
  for skin and face, 8–12
  for teeth, 12–13
 for illness
  for ailing adults, 70–78
  discontented babies, 54–55
  for nursery age children, 48–49
  sick children, 55–57
  preparation for childbirth, 80–81
  remedies for household pests, 93–94
Relishes, 130–132
Remember the Alamo (1898), 23
Respect for elders, 65
Respect for others, 64
Rice flour toilet soap, 11
Rickets, 58
Roast Goose recipe, 193
Royal Croquettes recipe, 169–170
Russian Tea recipe, 186

Sage, 79
Salad à la Red Devil recipe, 161
Salad recipes, 160–164
Sally Lunn recipe, 143
Salmon Croquettes recipe, 151
Sandwich Fillings for Picnics and Daytime Gatherings, 189–190
Saratoga Potatoes recipe, 156
Scalloped Cheese, Nice for Tea recipe, 187

[227]

Scrappel recipe, 149
Seasonal cooking tasks, 136–138
Seasonal soaps, 11
Seasonings, 130
Shirred Eggs in Shredded Wheat Biscuit Baskets recipe, 159
Sick children, 55–57
Sick room
  managing odors of, 68
  nursing management of, 67–69
  See also Illness
The Sighs of Love recipe, 183
Singleton, Phillip, 32
Skin care recipes, 8–10
Sleeping arrangements
  attending child at bedtime, 44
  in the outdoors, 93
  praying with children, 45
  rooms/bedding/clothing, 43–44
Sleeping rooms
  for children, 43–44
  decorating and furnishing, 92–93
  removing bedbugs, 94
Sloan, Earl S., 173
Sloan's Cook Book and Advice to Housekeepers (1905), 110, 169, 173, 193, 204
"The Small Belongings of Dress" (*The Ladies' Home Journal*, 1894), 13, 16
"Solid Days in Texas" (Powers), 77, 153
Soothing syrups, 55
Soup recipes, 165–167
A Southern Girl in '61—The War-Time Memories of a Confederate Senator's Daughter (1905), 54, 200
Spoonbread recipe, 141–142
Spring Chicken Tirolienne recipe, 172
Stoddard, Elizabeth, 14
Storeroom, 103–104
Stowe, Harriett Beecher, 119, 121, 122, 182, 186
"Studies in Cheerfulness—I" (1898), 127
"Styles of the Month for Children" *(McCall's Magazine)*, 50
Summer dinner desserts, 178
Summer menu, 163

Supper menu, 155
Swearingen, Patrick, 17, 87, 109, 205
Sweet Home Cook Book (1888), 164, 172, 175, 177, 186

Tact, 24
  See also Etiquette
Tamale Pie recipe, 150–151
Taste the Taste and Some Cookery News (1910s), 159, 161, 162
"Teaching Table Manners" (*Childrens Repository*), 66
The Tea-Party (Stoddard), 14, 90, 106, 188
Teas
  afternoon, 190
  breakfast, 144
  desserts for spring, 187
  preparing, 116–117, 186
  recipes for special occasion, 185–190
Teeth
  daily cleaning of, 7, 13
  recipes for care of, 12–13
Terrapin preparation, 125–126
Testicular pain remedy, 74
Texas for invalids/consumptives, 70
Thanksgiving Dinner *(Dr. Chase's...)*, 193
Thanksgiving Mince Pie recipe, 191–192
Tidy habits, 5
Tobin Drug Co. (advertisement), 73
Toilet supplies, 5
Toothache remedies, 57, 73
"To Texas, and By the Way" (Clifford), 28, 85
Traveling etiquette, 201–202
"The Two Lovers" (Cary), 30, 34, 68, 69

Unction de Mainteon, 10
Underclothing, 14

Vanilla, 79
Vanilla Ice Cream recipe, 180
Veal Loaf recipe, 149
Vegetables
  preparation of, 128–130
  recipes for, 153–158

[228]

Vegetable Soup with Dumplings recipe, 165
Venomous bite treatment, 72
Vielé, Teresa, 4
Violet powder recipe, 8
Visiting etiquette, 199–202
The Vital Question Cook Book (1908), 159

Watercress Sandwiches recipes, 190
The Way to a Man's Heart (1903), 161
Wedding Cake recipe, 194
Weekly baths, 5
What Mrs. Fisher Knows About Old Southern Cooking (1881), 167, 170, 175
"What Will You Have?" *(The Tea-Party)*, 188–189
What a Young Woman Ought to Know (1898), 18, 31, 51, 95
Wheaten Grits recipe, 49

Whipped syllabub recipe, 181–182
The White House Cook Book (1887), 198
White House diary (Hayes, 1878), 152
Whooping cough remedies, 56–57
Wilhelmina, Queen, 10
Winter Succotash recipe, 157–158
Wives
 advice for, 37–42
 hostess duties by, 195–198
 marriage and finance advice for, 41
 marriage and toiletry advice for, 39
 See also Mothers
W.M. Underwood Co., 162
Women. *See* 19th century Texas women
Woodward's Architecture and Rural Art (1867), 107
Wright's Book of 3000 Practical Receipts (1869), 94
Wrinkle cream recipe, 10–11

Yeast preparation, 115